ADULT PROBATION AND JUVENILE SUPERVISION

For Hooi

I couldn't have done it without you

Adult Probation and Juvenile Supervision
Beyond the Care – Control Dilemma

L R SINGER
Assistant Chief Probation Officer
Merseyside Probation Service

Avebury

Aldershot · Brookfield USA · Hong Kong · Singapore · Sydney

© L. R. Singer, 1989

All rights reserved. No part of this publication may be reproduced, stored in a retrieval system, or transmitted in any form or by any means, electronic, mechanical, photocopying, recording or otherwise without the prior permission of Gower Publishing Company Limited.

Published by

Avebury

Gower Publishing Company Limited,
Gower House, Croft Road, Aldershot,
Hants. GU11 3HR, England

Gower Publishing Company,
Old Post Road, Brookfield, Vermont 05036
USA

Printed and Bound in Great Britain by
Athenaeum Press Ltd., Newcastle upon Tyne.

HV
9278
.S57
1989

ISBN 0-566-07081-2

Contents

List of Tables		vii
Acknowledgements		ix
1	**Introduction**	1
	The Problem	1
	The Research	2
	Layout of the Book	6
	Notes	6
2	**Explanation**	7
	The Theme of Explanation	7
	Explaining Crime	8
	Explaining Care and Control	21
	An Alternative Typology of Aims	30
	A New Dilemma	38
	Notes	41
3	**Association**	44
	The Theme of Association	44
	Frequency of Contact	45
	Infrequency of Contact	52
	Location of Contact	60
	The Composition of Contact	65
	Notes	70
4	**Interaction**	72
	The Theme of Interaction	72
	Conversation	73
	Comprehension	80
	Conflict	88
	Notes	95

5	**Intervention**	96
	The Theme of Intervention	96
	Critical Incidents	97
	Strictness	110
	Breaching	116
	Notes	123
6	**Transformation**	125
	The Theme of Transformation	125
	General Findings	127
	Suspicion	128
	Employment	130
	Ostracism	131
	Damaged Self-Image	132
	Anti-Label/Labeller Reactions and Martyrdom	133
	Notes	135
7	**Conclusion**	136
	Towards a New Perspective for Probation Practice	136
	Theorectical Implications	138
	Practical Implications	139

Appendix
Probationer Interview Guide ... 147

Bibliography ... 158

List of tables

2.1	Explanations of crime	11
2.2	Officers' and probationers' explanations of crime	12
2.3	Probationers' social characteristics by officers' and probationers' orientations	18
2.4	Probationers' ages by officers' and probationers' orientations	20
2.5	Officers' and probationers' definitions of care	25
2.6	Officers' and probationers' definitions of control	25
2.7	Officers' and probationers' explanations of supervisory aims	31
2.8	Officers' and probationers' aims by type of offence orientation	32
2.9	Probationers' criminal history by the aims they mentioned	37
3.1	The average frequency of interviews for the initial and central phase quarters	46
3.2	Officers' aims and the frequency of contact with probationers	47
3.3	The probationers' characteristics and the frequency of contact during both quarters	50
3.4	The proportion of missed appointments for both quarters	53
3.5	The principal meeting arrangements for the initial and central quarters	61
3.6	Venue preferences during the central quarter according to gender	64
3.7	Venue preferences during both quarters according to age	65
3.8	The extent of groupwork contact	66
3.9	The attitude of participants toward groupwork	69
4.1	The top ten topics of conversation between officers and probationers	73
4.2	Who usually did the most talking	77
4.3	The probationers' understanding of the officers	81

vii

4.4	The officers' understanding of the probationers	85
4.5	Officers' supervisory aims and the proportion of disagreements reported	90
5.1	Incidents reported by officers and probationers in rank order	100
5.2	The officers' and probationers' evaluation of incidents	101
5.3	Officers' aims and the methods reported by them and the probationers	108
5.4	The officers' strictness in directing the probationers	111
5.5	The officers' strictness in monitoring the probationers	113
5.6	Officers' supervisory aims and the strictness of their routine surveillance	116
6.1	The consequences of people knowing the probationer was under supervision	127
6.2	Type of damaged self-image and reoffending	133

Acknowledgements

This book could not have been produced without the generous help of a number of people and organisations. In particular I would like to thank:-

Hooi, Lara and Luke Singer for their patience and encouragement;

The Centre for Socio-Legal Studies, Oxford, who gave me a studentship to undertake this research, and Wolfson College, Oxford, for covering the transcription costs of the fieldwork interviews;

The Berkshire officers and probationers who participated in the fieldwork and taught me about probation practice;

Doreen McBarnet for her stimulating (academic) supervision;

Pat Carlen, Juliet Cheetham, Mike Collison, Martin Davies and Roger Hood, each of whom contributed useful suggestions during the course of bringing this project to fruition;

My past and present probation colleagues in Berkshire and Somerset who have all assisted with the furtherance of my probation education, especially Judy Wilde during the write-up and Alan Croston in connection with publishing my ideas;

The Probation and Educational Research Trust, the Somerset Probation Committee, Somerset Probation and Community Enterprises and Tony Wells on behalf of the South West Regional (Probation) Staff Development Unit for their generosity in providing funding for the publication of this book.

1 Introduction

The Problem

This book is about a dilemma which threatens to undermine the future of probation practice. The dilemma derives from what is now customarily regarded as the probation officer's duality of role and the problem of having to simultaneously care for and control the offenders under their statutory supervision. Although those engaged in duelling with this dualism have defined it differently, most would probably agree with the summary of it offered by the Butterworth Committee resulting from their review of the work of the probation officer:

> The Probation Officer is an officer of the Court and personally accountable to it. In consequence, the relationship or nexus between the Probation Officer and client is based upon the client's involvement before the Court, rather than directly upon his social need. For this reason, the client is almost always in conflict with society, and the Probation Officer, in addition to establishing a relationship with him which aims at influencing attitude and behaviour, must represent to him the authority of the Court and endeavour to persuade him to accept it. The Probation Officer, in short, must consider the protection of society as well as the need and welfare of his client. The reconciliation of these objectives is often difficult and sometimes impossible (1972 p. 6).

Thus in order to work as a Probation Officer it is necessary to both care i.e. attend to the client's welfare, and control i.e. consider

1

society's protection. However, when these two elements are combined they are at best likely to be 'often difficult', and at worst 'sometimes impossible' to reconcile; the one vital constituent militating directly against the other. Nevertheless they must be combined because of the officer's role. Consequently it seems that, like schizophrenics imprisoned in a double bind (Bateson 1956), no matter what the probation officers do they cannot win.

If the Butterworth Committee neglected to offer any theoretical or practical solutions to this dilemma, then subsequent probation commentators have been eager to fill the vacuum. Throughout the seventies and eighties academics, policymakers and practitioners seem to have become trapped in an interminable debate about the problem's resolution: spurred on by the Younger Report's proposals for 'a new system of control in the community' (1974 para. 21); the Cullen v Rogers ruling about limiting 'the unfettered discretionary control of the probation officer' (1982 1 WLR 729); the 1982 Criminal Justice Act's strengthened probation orders intended to 'make real demands on offenders' (Home Office 1984 p. 21); and most recently, the Government's Green Paper 'Punishment Custody and The Community' (1988) with its suggestion of subjecting offenders supervised in the community to electronic tagging and tracking. Indeed the centrality and apparent intractibility of the dilemma was given its official seal recently when the Home Office Minister John Patten addressed the Association of Chief Officers of Probation and observed [1]:

> I acknowledge straightaway that there is an inherent tension between the concept of control - let alone punishment - and the roles of the probation service which are variously described as 'welfare', 'caring' or 'helping' - however these are defined.

The Research

The identification of this tension and the basic contradiction it represents for probation practice provided the focus for the research reported here. In addressing it however, instead of taking the existence of the problem for granted, the concepts giving rise to it were themselves treated as problematic. The evolution of this deliberately sceptical approach, in contrast to the credulous analyses traditionally preferred by care-control duellists, derived from posing three questions at the outset of the research. First, what precisely did the concepts of care and control mean when used as either an explanation of the idea of probation practice or as a description of the practice of the probation idea? Second, could the importance accorded to the care-control dilemma and, when taken to its logical conclusion, the potentially devastating consequences for probation practice, have been exaggerated out of all proportion by the Butterworth Committee and many other influential commentators? Put another way, if doing supervision is so difficult how come statutory orders continue to be made and supervised? Third, was there an alternative way of making sense of the sense made of probation practice by those either commentating on or participating in it?

To answer these questions a critical review of relevant probation commentary and research was undertaken i.e. the library-work. The results of this literature survey were then linked to new material elicited from a sample of participants directly engaged in doing supervision i.e. the field-work. Although a considerable amount of research into probation practice has been undertaken by the Home Office and various academic institutions, most of it relates only indirectly to the care-control dilemma. Hitherto, researchers have either examined the issue in passing as part of a more general project or focused on a particular aspect of it [2]. In both instances the information is tantalisingly partial. While the data is extremely useful as background material for putting the dilemma in context - as indeed it came to be used in the present research - it nevertheless seemed an unsatisfactory substitute for a systematically detailed scrutiny of what is entailed in doing supervision. Accordingly, an operational model of supervision conceived as a sequence of accomplishments was gradually devised and provided a framework for combining and analysing the results of the library- and field-work. The model comprises five themes concerned with the aims, methods and effects of supervision; namely explanation, association, interaction, intervention and transformation. Explanation examines the participants' account of crime and the supervisory responses following them; association, how their contact is organised; interaction, the nature of their relationship; intervention, the perceived helpfulness and strictness of the officers; and transformation, the degree of stigma experienced by the offenders. Each theme seeks to record sequentially the operation of supervision in relation to the definition and implementation of particular supervisory objectives and the specific problems commentators have claimed to attend them.

The sample consisted of fourteen probation officers, employed by Berkshire Probation Service, and eighty-four of their adult probation and juvenile supervision cases i.e. six probationers per officer [3]. Attention was paid to officers and probationers as well as adults and juveniles so as to make the fieldwork as comprehensive as possible. It was, however, confined to adult probation and juvenile supervision. This reflected the recognition that, while the Probation Service is involved in a number of other types of statutory supervision, it is probation and supervision orders which have attracted the most critical comment with respect to the care-control issue. Two main points about the sample need to be acknowledged. First, regarding their social characteristics, both the officer and the probationer groups were varied enough to permit statistical analyses of key factors implicated in care-control discourse to be undertaken [4]. The officers, for example, were evenly spread in relation to their age, gender, type of training and years of service. Similarly the probationers represented a useful cross-section in terms of their age, gender, type of offence, previous convictions, offence gravity and social class. To add to the diversity of the sample, the officers and probationers were drawn from two separate and contrasting locations; one serving a city and the other a market town [5]. Second, however, because of the relatively small number of cases sampled, it would be wrong to assume that they are wholly representative of the total population from which they were drawn. Further research will be necessary to verify or refute the findings derived from them. Nevertheless the view was taken that, for exploratory purposes, the sample was sufficiently large and heterogeneous to constitute a provisional - if not conclusive -

empirical contribution to a debate which has tended, in Fowler's apt words, 'to generate more heat than light' (1976 p. 158). In January 1981 the major fieldwork commenced and continued for nine months thereafter. Because of the wish to explore the experiences of current rather than closed cases, a quasi-longitudinal approach was adopted. Officers and a randomly selected group of their probationers were interviewed only after six months' supervision had elapsed - unless the supervision terminated earlier, in which case the interview was brought forward. Those cases with the longest duration were reviewed first and those with the shortest duration last so as to introduce consistency in the timing of the fieldwork. If a probationer became involved in breach proceedings after the fieldwork had been conducted then the case was followed-up and re-interviewed.

Ideally a fullblown longitudinal study would have been conducted; studying all new probation and supervision orders made in the two offices periodically from start to finish. However, this was not feasible for various reasons including the fact that these types of statutory order can vary from six to thirty-six months duration and time was not available for such an extensive period of fieldwork. Furthermore, to have waited until six new cases per officer became available would, because of the limited time available to undertake fieldwork, have resulted in an over-concentration of cases situated in the initial rather than central phase of supervision. This distinction between the initial and central phases of supervision is based on observations from previous probation commentary and research, as well as a review of closed case records undertaken in the two Berkshire offices prior to the major fieldwork. In Monger's analysis of probation practice, for example, he comments that although probation/supervision orders vary in length, they can nevertheless be divided into three distinguishable phases; namely the initial, the central and the terminal phases:

> one begins by focusing upon understanding (i.e. the first phase) proceeds to whatever solving of problems, dealing with difficulties, meeting of needs seems indicated (i.e. the central phase); and finishes by making sure that the client's dependence has been worked through so that by the time the order terminates, he is as self-reliant as possible.
> (1972 p. 56)

Empirical confirmation of this pattern can be noted in Folkard's (1974) adult probation and Giller and Morris' (1978) juvenile supervision studies. Both studies reported contact was greatest at the start of the order but that there was a,

> progressive decline in the number of interviews over a period of the probation order, and this was reflected in a similar pattern for other aspects of treatment.
> (Folkard op. cit. p. 5)

Similarly, from reviewing the closed case records, particularly the frequency of contact registered in the Part C's and the treatment plans described in the Part B's of the records, a definite shift from clarifying the purposes and rules of supervision to carrying out the treatment plans could be noted. Monger does not specify exactly when during the course of the order this shift occurs but both studies and the Berkshire records suggested that the transition from the initial to the central phase was usually no sooner than after the first month nor later than the six month stage. After this point the problems dealt with in the supervision were established and responded to by a distinctive style of work and frequency of contact which diminished gradually near the time of the order's expiry. Because the fieldwork plan was to research the aims, i.e. what Monger terms 'focusing upon understanding', as well as the methods and effects i.e. 'solving of problems', of probation/supervision orders, the initial and central phases seemed to be of crucial significance. Although it would have been more comprehensive to have examined all three phases, the terminal phase was not thought to be as relevant to the care-control issue as the preceding phases nor, given the time constraints on the fieldwork, as feasible to research as adequately as the first two phases. By staggering the interviews so that the oldest cases were reviewed first and the newest cases last, it was possible to interview all the probationers while they were in their central phase of supervision i.e. the average case duration was ten months.

Because the fieldwork pre-dates the passage of the Criminal Justice Act 1982 and the arrival of Schedule 11 probation and supervision orders, the material presented here might appear to be already out of date. However, while it is true that this research is unable to directly inform the care-control issue as it applies to these particular types of probation/supervision order, it is equally true that since their enactment Schedule 11 orders have only constituted a small minority of probation/supervision orders (Home Office 1986 [b] p. 41 and p. 52).

Given the multi-faceted nature of supervision it was thought appropriate to employ a multi-faceted set of methods and techniques to collect data from the sample. This involved interviews, case record analysis and observation. Because of the absence of a universally agreed checklist of probation practice, it was necessary to compile the contents of the Interview Guide incrementally by a process of trial and error [6]. This task was initiated by a survey of the literature, especially Carver (1974), Hardiker (1975), McEachern (1961) and various Home Office research studies. Subsequently and more substantially, however, the contents were derived from the formulation of the operational model of supervision described earlier and key variables emerging from the review of closed case records. Certain questions were piloted with officers during informal discussions which preceded the formal interviews. Eventually forty-one separate aspects of probation practice which could be related to the care-control issue were specified, leading to the generation of ninety-two questions in total (see Appendix).

The Interview Guide, in accordance with the principles of methodological triangulation (Denzin 1970), was also used as a framework for generating material from the case record reviews and observational work as well as for cross-checking data from one source with another. Because a wealth of material was collected it was possible to obtain data amenable to not only a qualitative but also a quantitative analysis. In this respect the variety of methods employed represent an attempt to reconcile what McBarnet (1978) has described as the neat yet separate corollaries of ethnographic and statistical approaches to criminal justice research.

Layout of the Book

In Chapters 2-6 the participants' perspectives are examined in detail according to the sequential model outlined above and, wherever possible, against the background of current knowledge. They show how, in spite of the pervasive reference to care and control, these concepts are more usefully regarded as ideological constructs concerned with prescribing what probation officers ought to do instead of explaining and describing what they actually do. An alternative typology of supervisory aims does however emerge from the participants' accounts in Chapter 2 and its applicability to probation practice is provisionally indicated on the basis of the material subsequently reviewed in Chapters 3-6. Finally, Chapter 7 draws together the various findings with direct reference to the theoretical and practical questions raised by this exploratory inquiry into doing supervision.

Notes

[1] Quoted in NACRO News Digest, November 1988 p. 23.
[2] Examples will be given in the following chapters.
[3] Henceforth the term 'probationer' will be used here as a convenient shorthand for all of the officers' cases.
[4] The particular statistical tests employed here were the Chi Square Test for the probationers and, because of the small number sampled, the Fisher Exact Test for the officers (Siegel 1956).
[5] Full details of the sample are available from L. Singer (1988) 'Doing Supervision: An Inquiry Into The Idea of Probation Practice And The Practice Of The Probation Idea' D. Phil thesis Oxford University.
[6] Apart from minor and obvious modifications the questions contained in the Interview Guide were the same for the officers and the probationers.

2 Explanation

The Theme of Explanation

Explanation is the stock in trade of the Probation Officer. Like social workers generally, the social work process in which the officer is engaged may be broadly summarised as entailing a commitment to,

> a deliberate widening of people's perceptions and understanding of the world in which they live with a view to an enhancement of their abilities to manage in it.
> (Butrym 1981 p. 90)

In the probation setting explanation has either been observed or is expected to encompass both the pre- and post-sentence work of the officer. More specifically, it involves explaining the causes of offences in social enquiry reports (Hardiker 1979), the effects of court orders (Probation Rules 1965 r.33), and subsequently helping the offender and society each 'to understand the other better' (Mathieson 1976). Within this process the probationer is regarded as a vital contributor. As the Morison Committee put it [1]:

> The caseworker must build gradually upon the individual's own account of himself, however incomplete or inarticulate... If the probationer feels free and has sufficient desire to explain and examine, with the caseworker's help, the feelings and attitudes which underlay or accompany his problem, or have made him a problem to society, he may be able, with continuing help, gradually to see himself and his place in society in a new and more mature way (1962 pp. 24-25).

How then do officers and probationers explain crime and the purpose of the supervisory responses to it? What exactly is the nature and relationship between these types of explanations? In spite of their importance, no systematically detailed examination of these questions based on both groups' views has been undertaken. Nevertheless commentaries and studies touching on such questions appear to hinge on three interlocking domain assumptions [2].

1. The justice and welfare perspectives (Parsloe 1976) provide officers and probationers with a general framework for explaining crime and the supervisory responses to it.

2. The concepts of care and control offer both groups a more accurate means of theorising the purpose of supervision than the traditional description of the officer's responsibility being to advise, assist and befriend the offender (Jarvis 1980).

3. Adherence to the justice perspective is associated with explaining crime and the supervisory response in terms of the absence of and therefore the need for control, while adherence to the welfare perspective is associated with explaining crime and the supervisory response in terms of the absence of and therefore the need for care.

These domain assumptions are adopted and assessed in the analysis that follows.

Explaining Crime

As Parsloe has observed in her discussion of the welfare and justice approaches to the British criminal justice system,

> Each approach differs in the explanation offered for criminal or delinquent behaviour and in the meaning said to be attributed by the offender to his entry into and progress through the system. These differences in beliefs about causation and meaning lead to, and are supported by, differences in what are regarded as the primary aims of the system. These in turn support different approaches to treatment or disposition, to the protection of rights or the meeting of need (op. cit. pp. 71-72).

It is not therefore, as might initially be thought, that a particular social work approach gives rise to a particular explanation of the offender's crime, but that both the offence and response to it are closely related to an over-arching orientation toward the criminal justice system i.e. the welfare and justice perspectives [3]. Consequently, commentators and researchers in the probation context have tended to refer to the welfare and justice perspectives or orientations, rather than the individual concepts of welfare and justice. As will be seen below, reference to the welfare and justice orientations, as distinct from concepts, has provided a useful basis for classifying officers' and probationers' explanations of crime. Unfortunately, however, the precise nature and distribution of these explanations as well as the link with their over-arching orientations remains uncertain. This is because, first, the number of detailed studies is negligible and second, the more detailed analyses, usually of officers' accounts, contain major conceptual contradictions. Broadly speaking, two approaches to the analysis of officers' explanations of crime can be identified and both seem prone to this problem of contradiction. For convenience these different approaches will be distinguished here as the factorial and typological approaches.

In the factorial approach attention is focused on the number of times various discrete factors are mentioned by officers as an explanation of offending. These are then aggregated to provide an overall impression of the officers' explanations. The disadvantage of this approach is that it can lead to an over concentration on particular factors at the expense of failing to acknowledge the different perspectives giving rise to them. Webb and Harris (1984) for example, from a content analysis of the social enquiry reports produced on a large sample of juveniles, suggest that probation officers explain juvenile delinquency in terms of pathological factors related to the breakdown of the 'family nexus'. Underpinning this analysis is the assumption that officers' explanations are welfare rather than justice oriented and the most popular factor identified i.e. 'significant separation from parents', would seem to confirm this. However, a major conceptual contradiction emerges when they report the second most popular factor. This we are told was 'problematic parental disciplining' and is a factor frequently cited as an element belonging to the justice perspective [4]. If these two causal factors are important constituents of officers' explanations, their differing theoretical origins remain unacknowledged and the overall conclusion that officers base their explanations solely on the welfare perspective is extremely misleading.

In the typological approach, this problem is overcome by grouping the diversity of perceived factors within a broader analytic framework of types which recognises the influence of the justice and the welfare perspectives. The problem here, however, concerns the accuracy of the types employed. Hardiker and Webb (1979) for example, from sampling eighteen officers' last five social enquiry reports concluded that, while a wide range of explanations were used by officers, two separate and distinct types of explanation could nevertheless be noted. These were the 'action' and the 'infraction' types of explanation and are directly associated with the welfare and justice perspectives. According to Hardiker and Webb the welfare oriented action explanation was the most popular type covering roughly two-thirds of the explanations given. This orientation views offence behaviour deterministically as,

> a reflection of a person's biological, psychological or social situation which makes law-breaking inevitable.
> (ibid. p. 15)

Conversely, the justice oriented infraction explanation thinks of criminality in voluntaristic terms as a legal status rather than personal characteristic:

People may embrace this status in specific situations either because they are caught on the invitational edge of opportunities to commit crimes and/or because they happen to have been caught by the Police (ibid. pp. 15-16).

Hardiker and Webb's marshalling of evidence is persuasive and seems to overcome the disadvantages of the factorial approach; but it runs into problems when a closer inspection of their findings is made. A point relegated to the footnotes leaves the reader struggling to resolve a major contradiction. If, as they maintain, officers' explanations can be understood by reference to these two distinctive types of explanation, how can it be that 'in many cases both infraction and action accounts were offered' [5]? What this contradiction seems to imply is that it is not so much the typological approach _per se_ but the particular types employed by Hardiker and Webb which is at fault; specifically that they do not provide sufficient typological precision to accommodate all of the officers' explanations.

It was for this reason that a typological rather than factorial approach was adopted, though with some important modifications to Hardiker and Webb's typology. Instead of restricting the typology to only two general types it was expanded to four more precise items. These attempted to incorporate not only the welfare/deterministic and justice/voluntaristic modes of explanation but also the psychological/internal and sociological/external variants also identified in the literature (Parsloe 1976, Sheppard 1980, and Tutt 1982). In the interests of simplicity, text book style definitions were set aside in favour of more everyday sounding descriptions. In Table 2.1 below the four types and their distinguishing orientation and focus are described. The intention of the typology was twofold. First, to provide sufficient variety and precision to avoid the contradiction noted in Hardiker and Webb. Second, to generate a means of linking the officers' and probationers' everyday accounts with the researcher's concern to theorise them both in terms of whether, on the one hand, they were justice or welfare oriented, and on the other, if they had a psychological or sociological focus.

Given the difficulties identified in other researchers' attempts to classify officers' views, a fifth open-ended option was added to the four types in anticipation of those respondents who might consider them inappropriate. In fact the typology proved sufficiently comprehensive and none of the sample opted for an alternative type of explanation. Moreover, not only were all the respondents willing and able to link their own explanations with the types, but in the process they each chose one rather than a plurality of types, thereby eliminating the problem of contradiction [6].

So how do officers and probations explain crime? Do they view it differently and, if so, in what way? In Table 2.2 below the officers' and probationers' explanations of crime are grouped according to the types preferred. If nothing else, the Table confirms the joint presence of the justice and the welfare orientations as the larger systems, as distinct from single system, of thought which constitute the background of both officers' and probationers' interpretations of offence behaviour.

Table 2.1
Explanations of crime

TYPE	ORIENTATION	FOCUS	DESCRIPTION
Pathologic	Welfare	Psychological	Although you knew the law your feelings and thoughts were mixed up because of personal problems and you couldn't help yourself.
Anomic	Welfare	Sociological	Some people you knew expected you to obey the law while others expected you to break it and it was hard to know what was right to do.
Calculative	Justice	Psychological	You believed in deciding for yourself what was right and wrong and it just turned out that this led to your doing something which broke the law.
Opportunistic	Justice	Sociological	You decided to take a chance and were unlucky getting caught doing what everybody else does or would do given the opportunity.

Table 2.2
Officers' and probationers' explanations of crime

TYPE	OFFICERS		PROBATIONERS	
	N	%	N	%
Pathologic	34	40.5	30	35.7
Anomic	11	13.1	8	9.5
Calculative	11	13.1	12	14.3
Opportunistic	28	33.3	34	40.5
	84	100	84	100

Looking more closely at the Table and taking into account the different foci of the explanations, there does appear to be a numerically slight though nonetheless radical difference between the two groups. Whereas the welfare oriented and psychologically focused pathologic explanation proved to be the most popular interpretation among the officers i.e. 40.5%, the justice oriented and sociologically focused opportunistic explanation was preferred by an identically large proportion of the probationers. However, although this would seem to confirm the claim made by some commentators that officers and probationers explain offending from diametrically opposed perspectives (Parker 1979, Walker and Beaumont 1981), a more detailed statistical analysis of Table 2.2 suggests stronger grounds for falsifying than verifying such a conclusion. If, for example, the four individual types of explanation chosen by the officers and probationers are correlated, no statistically significant association can be demonstrated (x^2 = 1.348, d.f.1, N.S.). Similarly, if the officers' and probationers' explanations are grouped according to either their welfare i.e. pathologic and anomic, or justice i.e. calculative and opportunistic, orientations, again no statistically significant association can be found (x^2 = 1.166, d.f.1, N.S.). The limitations of the present sample, outlined in chapter one, are such that the results discussed here, as indeed with the rest of the empirical findings reported later, cannot be considered conclusive. Nevertheless, they do perhaps provide a serious basis for questioning the conclusiveness of claiming the existence of diametrically opposed perspectives.

When they could be identified, the main differences to emerge between the officers' and the probationers' explanations tended in the majority of cases to be one of focus rather than orientation. For example, when a seventeen year old female was prosecuted for stealing jewellery to the value of £650 from members of her family the officer stated in his report:

> At the time she stole the rings she was in a mood generally antipathetic to the rest of the family brought on by what she saw as constant reproaches by her parents. There would appear to be an element of jealousy of her eldest brother and

second sister and of the success and approval which both have aroused in their parents.

going on to elaborate his pathologic reasoning during the fieldwork interview:

> She was stealing sort of symbols of other people's success 'cause she didn't feel that she'd achieved very much - they'd achieved quite a lot in life these other two but particularly the sister. She resented that. I don't think you really resent people unless you feel bad about yourself - you know, resent people really deep enough to consciously hurt them.

In contrast, while sharing the welfare orientation, the probationer concerned disagreed with the psychological focus, preferring to explain her actions in terms of succumbing to peer group pressure i.e. anomic reasoning:

> There was a few of us involved in it but I was the only one that was picked up... I think a lot of the time I take too much notice of other people. It's just that when people are egging you on to do things and you know they're doing it and you say 'No' then you get 'Oh chicken, haven't you got any bottle?'. So you do it, you don't really want to do it, but you just want to keep up with the rest of them.

Similarly a twenty-one year old male's burglary of an office and removal of £16.50 from a safe was considered by the officer to have been a purely voluntary act, set within the sociological context and influence of belonging to an opportunistic subculture i.e. opportunistic reasoning:

> He was just in that subculture where criminality was the lifestyle. I mean you didn't work and you drank quite heavily at weekends but you went out at night and took what you wanted and you made money that way.

Although the probationer shared the same justice orientation as the officer, he rejected the idea of subcultural influence, stressing that the burglary had been down to him alone i.e. calculative reasoning:

> P.: I was broke. I had no work. I'd heard about this safe and decided to have a go.
>
> L.S.: Was anyone else involved?
>
> P.: Yea but it was down to me. What I thought was 'No work, no money, better nick some then!'.

For many officer probationer pairs, however, the differences in focus tended to be minor and were often well within the parameters of the same types of explanations chosen. For example, in the pathologic explanation, officers and probationers did not always agree on the precise nature or description of the determining factor but the psychological focus nevertheless remained. Among the officers, explanations tended to be expressed in clinical terms and were usually framed within the vocabulary of therapy (May 1971); viewing the offences as presenting symptoms of underlying problems. In order of the frequency mentioned, officers interpreted the offences as conscious or unconscious attention seeking gambits i.e. the classic crime as a cry for help:

> I think his not being in work had upset him and disturbed him but I think it was much more deep seated than that. I think it was the feeling of not having the attention that he wanted from his parents. I think he had this need to attract their attention.
> (18 year old male prosecuted for stealing £500 from his father's pub).

the manifestation of suppressed interpersonal difficulties:

> I think it's related to the family side, the invalid wife. If he hadn't suppressed his feelings and communicated them he wouldn't have cracked in this way. In an odd way he was punishing her; giving her gifts that he knew he hadn't paid for, that he had stolen, which he knew would horrify her no end. It's a reversal of the shoplifting woman who punishes her husband because there are problems in the marriage.
> (43 year old male prosecuted for a series of shop thefts to the value of £240).

and feeling rejected:

> Anger with his ex-girlfriend primarily, a deep sense of bitterness and great difficulty with coping with the fact that she was replacing him with someone else.
> (24 year old male prosecuted for criminal damage to the value of £10 as a result of damaging his ex-girlfriend's property).

For their part the probationers were inclined to be more emotive than clinical but nevertheless retained the psychological focus and the idea that their behaviour had arisen through internal factors beyond their immediate control. In order of frequency these were depression, desperation and compulsion:

> I'd had a few drinks. I went in the betting shop and 'er I had me two weeks' dole money. Anyway I went out the betting shop to get a bottle of cider, went back in there and done all me money - me two weeks' keep - and I got depressed. So I was drinking this cider in the betting shop and the manager behind the counter said 'Don't drink your cider in here!' and I was depressed losing me money. He was giving me a lot of mouth and I just rammed the bottle sideways and it went straight through the pane.
> (39 year old male prosecuted for criminal damage to the value of £7).

> I had no one to talk to. I couldn't go to my manager and say 'Look could you lend me some money until the end of the month?', I just didn't have it in me and I was upset because of my mother rejecting me and I couldn't go home to my step family. I had nowhere to go really but I had to get the

money to pay my rent.
(19 year old female prosecuted for stealing £57 from her employer).

It became a very very bad habit, it became a way of life eventually, I felt if I wasn't doing it something was gravely missing. Whether it was in a big way or a small way, it didn't matter. I mean it could be just a packet of sweets or it could be a tape recorder, it wasn't necessary because I wanted it or I wanted to eat it. It was just for the sake, for the sole purpose of taking things.
(36 year old prosecuted for series of thefts from shops to a value of several thousand pounds).

Regarding the justice oriented and sociologically focused opportunistic explanation, the officers' and probationers' accounts displayed a much greater level of congruence; the common denominator often being a blend of boredom and opportunity. For example a sixteen year old male probationer explained:

We was looking in the window and we sort of goes 'Oh I'd like that and I'd like that' and then it clicked, why don't we break in? So we went on top of the roof and had a spy round to see if we could get in there and we did. We just did it, you know boredom. Most of it's boredom. So I went out and done something with me mate, a bit of action.

His officer concurred:

The offence happened during the school holidays with a friend. They took watches, calculators and £75 in cash. Long boring school holidays are a great temptation to do something exciting and this was easy pickings.

Where differences between the officers and probationers were noted the variations again tended to be minor and did not overstep the boundaries of the opportunistic type of explanation. Differences usually arose over the emphasis given to either the excitement or the opportunity element, with no significant group preferences emerging. Sometimes the officer stressed the excitement element while the probationer emphasised the opportunity; at other times the position was reversed. For example, whereas two of the probationers involved in the same series of car thefts both emphasised how taking the vehicles had provided a 'cheap and convenient way of getting around', as well as an opportunity 'to earn some cash on the side' by selling the contents taken from the cars, the officer stressed the excitement element. In her report she wrote:

The immediate cause of the offending amounts to boredom. After one or two occasions taking cars became an alternative to spending an evening in the pub, and gave more excitement. The greatest excitement apparently came when the risk was greatest, that was actually getting into the cars and driving away or when the police were in sight... Even being in the police cells, to begin with at least, was exciting because it was different.

Conversely, another officer considered a fifteen year old male's spate of thefts from cars to have been purely opportunist. The juvenile concerned however stressed the excitement of risk-taking and competing with his friends rather than the actual cash and valuables he had been able to accumulate:

> It was sort of a period we were going through, like see who could go out and nick the most in a night. It seemed to be like this competition.

Differences between officers and probationers were therefore much less marked than might have been expected, being more frequently about the focus of the orientation rather than between the orientations themselves. This is not however to deny that there were instances of a major division of opinion but, as noted earlier, they were relatively infrequent and by no means one way. The argument, for example, that probationers were fighting a rearguard action against the encroachments of officers' patho-logic could not be upheld because officers could be as anti-pathology as the probationers, just as the probationers could be just as pro-pathology as the officers.

> He's a homosexual who is attracted very much, very strongly to younger boys and he has no control over his actions.

> What I did with the boy didn't seem wrong morally. My offences have always been because the person said yes. (Indecent assault on a 14 year old).

> She took a chance and probably thinks herself unlucky getting caught. I wouldn't accept it was 'A' (pathologic) that she was in such a financial muddle that she couldn't help herself.

> I think the Probation Officer thinks I'm stronger than I am. I was very vulnerable, getting beat up by my husband and not getting enough money. It was the whole upheaval of things. (Defrauding D.H.S.S.).

To complete the analysis of which particular types of explanation officers and probationers most frequently chose when explaining crime, it also seemed worthwhile to examine which particular officers and probationers most frequently chose certain types of explanation. Thus through inverting the focus of the analysis from the type-identified-by-the-person to the person-identified-with-the type it becomes possible to consider those, if any, social characteristics among both groups which were associated with and possibly influential in determining the choices made. Was it the case regarding officers, for example, that the apparently eclectic pattern suggested in Table 2.2 obscured a pattern within a pattern of them being individually committed to either a welfare or a justice oriented explanation of crime? This possibility is certainly implied by some commentators (Harris 1977 and 1980, Limont 1976 and Griffiths 1982). In fact what was apparent collectively proved to be evident individually and therefore both accords with and extends Hardiker and Webb's finding that officers as a group 'do not employ an all embracing monolithic model of deviance' (op. cit. p. 2). Only one officer displayed an exclusive commitment to one orientation alone. Furthermore, even if the instances of welfare/justice bias are taken into account i.e. where officers displayed a preference in two-thirds or more of their cases, this still only raised the biased number to just over half of the officers e.g. five being welfare and three being justice oriented. With such small numbers, specifying the presence or absence of distinguishing social characteristics such as age, gender, type of training or length of service has to be extremely tentative. Nevertheless the data did seem to suggest that, whether comparing the welfare with the justice biased or the biased with the unbiased, the particular officer characteristics reviewed were sufficiently mixed to elude statistical significance and were not associated nor therefore influential [7]. Indeed the most striking feature of the officers as a group was their eclecticism and how, independent of their social characteristics, instead of operating with a single orientation which they inflexibly took to each of their cases, they preferred instead to take each case to the two orientations they had at their disposal. This point is highlighted by two of the officers, one with a welfare bias and the other with a justice bias, who both happened to be supervising two pairs of probationers convicted of the same offence. In the first pair which involved offences of criminal damage and shoplifting by two brothers, the welfare biased officer refused to explain their offences in identical terms, preferring instead to attach a pathologic explanation to one and an opportunistic reason to the other:

> Attention seeking nervous boy. I should think he was looking for what he got frankly, supervision.

> I think there was a subcultural bit in it, he's a plucky, spunky sort of kid and I think at that age in his life stealing is a big temptation.

Similarly the officer with the justice bias thought the reasons why two friends had engaged in shoplifting to have been quite different i.e. calculative for one and pathologic for the other:

> I don't think he was at all mixed up and I would suspect that he didn't feel that guilty about being dishonest. I would think "C" applies (calculative); he made the decision and it led to something which broke the law. He has a fairly deep seated anti-authority streak, he's quite rebellious.

> I think he was a very unhappy boy. Previous attempts to run away from home. They were really signals that said 'Look I'm unhappy, someone take notice of the fact' and I think the shoplifting was perhaps another incident which was designed to do that, a cry for help or for attention of his plight, all sort of unconscious.

Table 2.3
Probationers' social characteristics by officers' and probationers' orientations

CHARACTERISTICS		TYPE OF ORIENTATION			
		Officers		Probationers	
		Justice	Welfare	Justice	Welfare
Gender	Male	31	33	37	27
	Female	8	12	9	11
		$x^2 = .438$, d.f. 1, N.S.*		$x^2 = 1.006$, d.f. 1, N.S.	
Class	Middle	12	15	17	10
	Working	27	30	29	28
		$x^2 = .055$, d.f. 1, N.S.		$x^2 = 1.074$, d.f. 1, N.S.	
Offence Gravity**	Low	12	9	13	8
	Medium	15	23	21	17
	High	12	13	12	13
		$x^2 = 1.73$, d.f. 2, N.S.		$x^2 = .899$, d.f. 2, N.S.	
Criminal History***	Low	22	20	26	16
	Medium	13	19	17	15
	High	4	6	3	7
		$x^2 = 1.199$, d.f. 2, N.S.		$x^2 = 3.382$, d.f. 2, N.S.	

*   N.S. means not statistically significant.

**   The criteria used to determine the offence gravity was based on Webb and Harris' (1984) coding.

***   Criminal history was classified as low where there were no previous offences, medium if there were between 1 and 2, and high if there were 3 or more.

If the officers' own social characteristics were not associated with the type of orientation chosen, could those of the probationers be significant? Investigating the officers' and probationers' distribution of explanations with this question in mind produced two surprising results. The first was the absence of associations where commentators and researchers would lead one to expect them. Worrall (1981), for example, argues convincingly that officers' orientation toward females differs markedly to their orientation toward males, with a much greater likelihood that officers will regard the criminal behaviour of females as pathological. However neither the officers nor the female probationers displayed such a bias to a statistically significant degree as Table 2.3 above indicates. Similarly, commentators from contrasting political positions have argued that officers tend to think the criminality of working-class probationers in welfare rather than justice terms i.e. either to unwittingly cool out potential protest (Walker and Beaumont 1981), or relieve social distress where it is greatest (Day 1981). Again though, as Table 2.3 shows, the distribution of the officers' and the probationers' explanations suggests such an association is statistically insignificant.

An even more striking surprise in this vein, given the positive research findings reported by Hardiker and Webb (op. cit.), was the absence of a statistically significant association between either the gravity of the offence or criminal history of the probationers and the orientation of the explanations preferred. Thus, whereas Hardiker and Webb found that the more serious the offence and criminal history of the probationer the more likely the officers were to explain the offence in action/welfare oriented terms, Table 2.3 demonstrates no such association for either the officers or the probationers. How can these differences with previous commentaries and research be explained? Earlier it was noted how officers did not apply a single orientation to all of their cases; instead applying each case to the orientations at their disposal. From the review of gender, class, offence gravity and criminal history, it would seem that we can now add to this the observation that the officers also do not appear to apply a pre-selected orientation to the probationers' offending based on their social characteristics. Indeed the same can be said for the probationers themselves i.e. there is no association between their social characteristics and the type of explanation to which they refer. This represents not only a substantive but also a methodological and theoretical departure from previous commentaries and research. Thus methodologically, commentators addressing the class and gender factors have arrived at conclusions based on impressionistic data which, while useful in suggesting the possibility of a relationship, when examined statistically is, so far as the present sample is concerned, now shown to be much less significant than regarded hitherto. Similarly, from a theoretical standpoint, had Hardiker and Webb employed a typology of greater precision it is conceivable that a lack of association would have been demonstrated; especially bearing in mind that, for gravity, nearly a fifth of their cases, and for criminal history, over a third of them, had to be excluded from the test of association because they could not be classified (op. cit. pp. 10-11).

There was however one exception to this general pattern of non-association and it brings us to the second surprising result. According to Parsloe (1979), the offences committed by juveniles are more susceptible to a welfare oriented type of explanation than those committed by adults 'because of their developing and immature state'. This is not to deny that the criminal behaviour of some adults can and is taken by officers as a sign of immaturity, but Parsloe articulates an assumption shared by many commentators that, on balance, more juvenile than adult offenders are likely to have their offences explained in welfare terms [8]. If we recall the distribution of explanations summarised in Table 2.2 it seems logical therefore to expect that an association would be found in the form of officers preferring a pathologic explanation for the juveniles and an opportunistic one for the adults. Moreover, given the similarity rather than difference in perception between officers and probationers already identified, we could also expect the probationers to view their offences in the same way. Paradoxically, although a statistically significant association was approached by the officers and reached by the probationers, it was in fact in the opposite direction to that expected. As Table 2.4 below shows, the pathologic type of explanation was more associated with the adults, while the opportunistic type was much more likely to be applied to or chosen by the juveniles.

Table 2.4
Probationers' ages by officers' and probationers' orientations [9]

	OFFICERS		PROBATIONERS	
AGE	Pathologic	Opportunistic	Pathologic	Opportunistic
Adults	24	13	27	13
Juveniles	10	15	3	21
	34	28	30	34

x^2 = 3.724, d.f. 1, P < 0.10 x^2 = 18.221, d.f. 1, p < 0.001

Three conclusions can be drawn from this unexpected distribution of explanations and refer to both the general findings obtained her as well as previous commentary and research. First, the distribution reinforces the point that the majority of officers and probationers tended to explain the offences similarly. The assumption of some commentators that officers and probationers subscribe to diametrically opposed perspectives simply has not stood the test of empirical scrutiny. Second, regarding probationers, researchers like Parker (1979) would seem to be right to claim that juvenile offenders tend to bring a justice instead of welfare orientation to their offending, but wrong to assert that probation officers do not do so also. This is because when the officers' explanations were actually recorded and compared with the probationers' - rather than being taken for granted - the evidence could not substantiate the assumption that they preferred a welfare to a justice orientation. Third, regarding officers, given the lack of statistically significant association, it would be quite mistaken to assume that when addressing a juvenile's offending they operated exclusively to the equation juvenile offence = welfare oriented explanation, or for that matter, juvenile offence = justice oriented explanation. In theorising the officers' explanations of crime, the key to analysing them appears to be a recognition of the commitment to neither a justice nor a welfare orientation but both, underscored by a process of personalisation whereby each case is interpreted according to its particular circumstances. In short, officers' explanations are personalised, taking neither a single explanation nor probationer characteristic as an a priori basis for explanation. However, their personalised mode of explanation is not free floating but set within the parameters of the justice and welfare orientations and their various foci.

Later in this chapter the relationship between these differing orientations to crime and the supervisory aims thought to be appropriate responses to them will be examined. Beforehand however, we need to clarify what, so far as officers and probationers are concerned, the supervisory aims actually are. In their review of the various methods of classification employed by criminologists, Hood and Sparks observe:

> Classification always reflects some purpose and one method of classification is 'better' than another only in respect of some particular purpose or purposes (1972 p. 124).

To what extent are the concepts of care and control 'better' in meeting the purpose of classifying officers' and probationers' understanding of supervisory aims than the often rehearsed description that the aim of supervision is to advise, assist and befriend the offender?

Explaining Care and Control

To assess whether the concepts of care and/or control could be meaningfully applied as a designation of the aim or aims of supervision, officers and probationers were asked to assess the purpose of their supervision in terms of whether it entailed caring about personal difficulties and/or controlling what probationers did or said so that they did not misbehave. These descriptions of the concepts were not intended to be definitive but rather to act as catalysts in focusing the officers' and probationers' minds on elaborating their own understanding of the concepts, something hitherto omitted by commentators and researchers alike. Bearing in mind the ambiguity surrounding the concepts generated in current probation commentary, it was anticipated that the elaborations derived would provide for a practically instead of polemically informed explanation of exactly what the concepts meant to those directly involved, whether or not they could be meaningfully applied to supervision and, if so, in what way [10]. Had the concepts become as Thorpe et al have argued, empty cliches that have 'outlived their usefulness' (1980 p. 97), or could their credibility be revived by starting afresh with them from the participants' perspective?

Ironically, eliciting the officers' and probationers' understanding of the concepts served more to reinforce than reject the ascription of them as cliches. Taken together, six different kinds of problem with the concepts were either perceived or presented by the majority in the process of considering and elaborating what the concepts of care and control meant to them as a designation of supervisory aims:-

1. Inaccuracy   i.e. the concepts were misleading.
2. Inadequacy   i.e. the concepts were too general as a description.
3. Variation   i.e. the concepts were defined so diffusely as to be incomprehensible.
4. Conflation   i.e. the concepts were not easily distinguishable from each other.
5. Confusion   i.e. where one concept was presented in terms traditionally associated with the other.

6. Prescription i.e. where the concepts denoted an ethical judgment of what supervisory aims ought to be instead of specifying what they actually were.

Although documented here separately, many of these problems overlapped with each other and in illustrating them below their isolation may sometimes appear artificial. For example, solutions to problems 1. and 2. often led to problem 3., which itself was closely associated with problems 4. and 5. There was not however any linear relationship from problem 1. through to problem 5. Instead the problems should be seen as contributing, each in their own particular way, to the difficulties the officers and probationers either confessed to experiencing, or by their accounts inadvertently fell victim to, when designating supervisory aims according to the vocabulary of care and control.

Inaccuracy

For just over a third of the officers i.e. five, the idea of aiming to care about probationers' personal difficulties and/or control what they did or said was simply inaccurate. Two officers took issue with both concepts because they considered them to divert attention away from instead of focusing upon their understanding of supervisory aims. One of the officers explained:

> I dislike the word caring intensely. It's wishy washy watery has all the dangers of do-gooding attached to it and I think that it's a sort of professionalised word which is really misleading. My own view is that if you want to talk about the aims of supervision you need a more accurate description. Wanting to care about personal difficulties is about wanting to be involved and being involved is about wanting to counsel, wanting to help. So care is a word that I'm very skeptical of. Control? Again the client always has the last laugh. I think that any social work intervention can be thrown back in the social worker's face because the client in the last resort is self-determining. Sure I instruct them to abide by the conditions of their orders and check out they're doing so but I don't try and control what they do or say in some Big Brother way.

The three remaining officers either rejected or required a major modification to the concept of control because, like the officer above, they also thought it was misleading. For these officers the idea of controlling what probationers did or said so they did not misbehave was 'not on' because it connoted physically controlling the probationer's behaviour. This was not considered feasible and therefore accurate as an aim:

> I think there is a lot of fantasy around about how much control a P.O. has. It is very little. Most of the offences committed by our seventeen to twenty-five age group are often when the landlords call time, he's got a lot of beer inside him, and when somebody whispers in his ear that such and such is a good idea, there's no probation officer at the other

22

elbow tugging his sleeve and saying it isn't. What you tell
the chap at four o'clock in the afternoon or what he tells
you the next time, hopefully has a knock-on effect but we are
really in the spin-off game rather than the direct-result
game.

Echoes of these sentiments were also voiced by a few of the
probationers i.e. eight or just under a tenth of them. Four
dismissed control, two rejected care and two others found both
concepts wanting. All of these criticisms were along similar lines
to those expressed by the following probationer, where Harris' (1980)
definition of care as demonstrating concern for the client's
wellbeing, and Griffiths' (1982) formulation of control as the
exercise of containment, are both considered inapplicable:

> P: I don't think it's either of them. I mean I've been
> down here sometimes, admittedly without an appointment,
> wanting to see my probation officer 'cause it was
> important like but couldn't 'cause she wasn't free. If
> it was the case that they cared for you as an
> individual, she would have given me ten minutes say, but
> she didn't she had to go to a meeting. I had to either
> wait till next week or come in when she had time so I
> don't think it's that.
>
> L.S: What about controlling what you do or say so you don't
> misbehave.
>
> P: I don't think that applies. Being on probation won't
> stop you misbehaving will it 'cause you only come here
> once a week say, for an hour and then the rest of the
> week I mean you can misbehave if you want.

<u>Inadequacy</u>

A less extreme, though nonetheless persuasive criticism, made by just
over another third of the officers, i.e. five, concerned the
adequacy of the concepts in explaining their aims. Here the problem
centred not so much on misrepresenting as understating their
supervisory plans. For these officers both concepts could be applied
to their supervisory aims, depending on the case under review, but
were too basic a description to specify their particular aims with
each case satisfactorily. One officer's observation was typical:

> It's a very basic description. As a generalisation I
> suppose it's fairly accurate but an awful lot more goes on
> between an officer and a client than those descriptions
> imply, besides it varies so much from client to client.

Another agreed and elaborated:

> The caring side is providing help which reduces a person's
> propensity to offend and I think that's about reducing
> whatever their painful pressures are. If they're external

ones you either try and take the pressure away or you do something to change the way they think about that pressure. I think supervision is also about conditional freedom and that's where the control comes in. There are two sorts of control I try and operate. Negative control, you know, it's to say don't do certain things, certain limited easily definable things and if you don't nothing bad will happen to you. There's also positive control, having the client report to you and account for himself with letters being wrote and sanctions brought if he doesn't.

Although among the probationers inaccuracy rather than inadequacy was the most frequently mentioned type of criticism, three of the probationers did consider the concepts to be inadequate. For one, both were 'a pretty watered down version' of what supervision was supposed to be, while the other two thought either care or control too general:

I know my P.O. cares about me but I'm not a child anymore. She doesn't care about me like that. She's not like my mum (laughs). She sort of makes suggestions and lets me get on with it.

He doesn't try and control what I do or say exactly. He asks you what you've been doing. I mean if I say I did something and it was wrong he tells me I shouldn't have done it. You can say he tries to control me that way.

Taken together therefore, over 70% of the officers and 13% of the probationers expressed dissatisfaction and in the process implied serious theoretical problems with the concepts. However, this still left nearly a third of the officers and a very substantial number of the probationers apparently sympathetic toward the concepts. Could therefore the elaborations provided by those either sympathetic toward or indeed critical of the concepts establish a basis for piecing together a more accurate and adequate definition of care and control as a designation of supervisory aims? Ironically, the problems with the elaborations presented were even more telling than the problems perceived.

<u>Variation</u>

The first problem common to all the officers' and probationers' elaborations revolved around the diversity instead of uniformity of the definitions given. Pinpointing a pair of core meanings was therefore frustrated by the diffuseness of these definitions when they were aggregated, being more indicative of conceptual chaos than clarity. In Tables 2.5 and 2.6 a representative sample of the officers' and probationers' definitions, quoted verbatim, is provided to illustrate the range of responses and problems encountered.

Table 2.5
Officers' and probationers' definitions of care

OFFICERS	PROBATIONERS
- Developing trust to share things. - Helping to divert from further trouble. - Helping to find greater happiness. - Enabling personal development. - Showing the person you are concerned by assisting them. - Taking account of individual peculiarity and needs, listening sympathetically and advising.	- Having someone to confide in. - Being given guidelines so you don't go down the wrong path. - Help with difficulties like paying in fines and explaining legal things. - Help with reading trouble and finding a job in the papers. - Someone to help you understand what you did wrong.

Table 2.6
Officers' and probationers' definitions of control

OFFICERS	PROBATIONERS
- Anything to do with making someone do something which they otherwise would not necessarily do. - Exercising through the medium of a relationship what your expectations as a probation officer are. - Keeping an eye on their behaviour. - Making sure and following up that the client keeps to the conditions of the order. - Using a framework, limits, demands.	- An eye over your shoulder all the time to see what you're doing. - Making me go down to the office. - Telling me my rights and my wrongs. - To keep a check on you, to find out what you're doing to try and direct you into something different if it's illegal.

As summary explanations of supervisory aims these statements were very instructive and later in this chapter their implications for an alternative typology of aims will be considered, but for the moment let us examine their consequences for the concepts of care and control. If as Lacey has argued 'to have a concept of anything is to be able to distinguish it from other things' (1979 p. 34), what the two Tables would seem to demonstrate is the presence of not one but a series of separate and distinct definitions of both care and control. Similarities may be noted, for example, between an officer's definition of care as 'listening sympathetically and advising' and a probationer's explanation of it as 'having someone to confide in', but is either definition the same thing as 'showing the person you are concerned about them by assisting them', or giving them 'help with reading trouble'? Rather than one there would seem to be two separate objectives implied here. Similarly regarding the concept of control, when an officer spoke of making the probationer 'do something which they otherwise would not necessarily do', a parallel could be drawn with the observation of one of the probationers that control meant 'making me go down to the office', but again is this the same thing as 'keeping an eye on their behaviour' or having 'an eye over your shoulder all the time'? Once more two distinguishable objectives would seem to be implied here. Aggregating the definitions of either care or control consequently proved unsuccessful because of the problem of variation which the concepts inspired.

Conflation

Another problem found with the officers' and probationers' elaborations related to their difficulty in distinguishing the two concepts from each other. For example, among the four officers sympathetic to the concepts as an explanation of their supervisory aims, two confessed to being unable to separate care from control, saying they found the attempt 'messy'. Interestingly, this view was expressed by an officer at the start of his career and an officer with over ten years experience; suggesting the difficulty was intrinsic to the concepts rather than influenced by the length of service of the officer and his exposure to the problem. The novice for example stated:

> If control has any real meaning it's controlling people through the use of a relationship whereby they feel obliged to look at their behaviour and the reasons that you disapprove of it. That's the relationship in it's most idealistic sense and I doubt very much that there are very many relationships of that ilk around but it certainly throws into relief the idea of caring and controlling being separate entities. I feel a lot of probation officers set out to use a relationship in a caring sort of way but unbeknown to them they're also using it in a controlling way. It all depends on the motives and purpose of each particular case and the whole thing gets quite messy.

Similarly the veteran claimed:

> I don't see the two as being that distinct and that separate. Control in a positive way has a very big element of caring in it and in the same way a crucial element of caring for someone is in fact directly influencing their behaviour in a way which you think is going to be good and beneficial for them. To me to cut the two things up into separate compartments is less than helpful and I think people get themselves into an unnecessary mess.

That other officers found distinguishing the concepts from each other messy was graphically illustrated on many occasions when, in discussing particular cases, they often inadvertently conflated the concepts even though they were deliberately attempting to draw a line between them! For example, when describing the case of a fourteen year old convicted of a burglary that occurred while truanting from school, one of the officers sympathetic to the concepts explained:

> My main objective is to control what he does because I can see that if he doesn't go to school he won't get a good

report and with the job situation as it is he won't get a
good job. I'm trying to control him because that's what his
aim is, to get a good job, which as far as I'm concerned is
his ticket for avoiding any more burglaries. So it's an
attempt to control him by getting him to go to school, which
he hates, because I'm caring about what happens to him. The
two things are sort of synonymous.

Not only did this officer conflate the two concepts but also in the process switch from Hunt's (1964) controlling-care model to Winnicott's (1962) caring-control version; all at the expense of providing for a consistent way of distinguishing either concept from the other. Although the officer's aim initially appears to be to get the juvenile to go to school so as to eventually get a good job i.e. controlling-care, it later transpires that getting a good job is intended to prevent him from getting into further trouble i.e. caring-control. It is important to note that this blurring of the conceptual boundaries was not an isolated instance and many of the probationers, like the officers, also found it hard to separate the concepts. As one complained to the researcher when pressed to distinguish them:

To my mind caring and controlling is near enough the same
thing. They try and control you by looking round and trying
to find you a job and say 'Look here's a job, go on', they've
rung up about it and want you to go there; that's the only
way they control you which is caring isn't it?

Confusion

A further problem with the concepts emerging from both groups' elaborations follows directly on from the problem of conflation and involves the confusing presentation of the two concepts in terms traditionally associated with the other. It can be recalled for example that some of the officers and probationers defined care as 'helping to divert from further trouble' or 'being given guidelines so you don't go down the wrong path'. If the emphasis is placed on the helping part of the aim it may, by a small stretch of the imagination, be possible to retrieve the definition from the terrain traditionally associated with control. But what are we to make of the following definition of control as an example of care, offered by another officer?

Some officers argue that by putting up with all sorts of
failure on the part of the client to report or comply with
the terms of the order they are demonstrating that they are
actually caring for them. Frankly I don't agree with that, I
think it's the other side of the coin, I think that that
basically demonstrates a lack of care rather than real care.
Real care is actually demonstrated by saying 'Look, you know
this is what you've got to do, these are your obligations'.

Or for that matter this officer's definition of care as an example of control?

In the caring relationship you try and find out what the
person's difficulties are, where they can't cope and have

been unable in the past to control themselves well: then to
help them to control it in future you point out to them and
on some occasions you actually step in and say 'Don't do that'.

Just under a quarter of the probationers i.e. twenty, confused the
traditional meanings of the concepts. Like the officers they were
mostly in the direction of seeing control as an example of care:

> Being a guardian to me, to keep an eye on you to find out
> that everything's alright at home. To see that you're
> alright in your own mind and you're quite happy about the
> situation you're in.

> Making me toe the line, to be careful when I go out drinking
> that I don't get too drunk and do something stupid.

However, a few of the probationers i.e. six, did cite certain
instances of what one might expect them to regard as care, as
examples of control:

> He says going to school can be a way for me to improve
> myself. So you could say he's caring about me but I think
> that for him to care he must want me to do something that's
> right for him so it's control.

> She's helped me out with my bills, the controlling was
> phoning up a few places and making arrangements for me to pay
> so much a week - of my electric for instance - so I didn't
> get cut off.

Such conceptual slippage, given the problems of variation and
conflation, is hardly surprising; but when these three limitations
are added together they provide compelling grounds for dispensing
with the concepts. Before doing so however it is useful to briefly
acknowledge a final problem which, through its discovery, offered the
researcher a clue to the puzzling persistence of the concepts in the
face of their manifest lack of conceptual unity and consistency.

Prescription

Since the time of Weber (1949) the view that social scientists need
to avoid making value judgments in their analyses has had a
checkered history. Some have disputed the possibility while others
the desirability (Blackburn 1972) but, in the sphere of social work,
combining the ethical with the theoretical appears to be a necessary
problem. The reason for this seemingly contradictory situation are
suggested by the C.C.E.T.S.W. working party's definition of a value:

> A value determines what a person thinks he ought to do,
> which may or may not be the same as what he wants to do, or
> what it is in his best interest to do, or what in fact he
> actually does. Values in this sense give rise to general
> standards and ideals by which we judge our own and others'
> conduct; they also give rise to specific obligations.
> (1976 p. 14)

Thus values are vital to social work because without them it is deprived of the standards and ideals which make it possible: but they are a necessary problem because they concern what the worker ought to do which may not be the same as what he is actually doing. This is precisely what appeared to happen with just under two-thirds of the officers i.e. nine, when invited to elaborate what they understood by the concepts of care and control. Instead of employing the concepts as a means of specifying what they actually planned to accomplish, the concepts were referred to in a manner more akin to the making of value judgments about what they ought to be aiming to achieve. This was especially noticeable with the concept of care as the following extracts indicate:

> I think that's why I'm in the job, to care about individuals with personal difficulties. I would say fundamentally I'm there to help people find greater happiness.

> Caring about personal difficulties is really about a will, a decision to love in the Christian or Judaistic sense of the word. That's my understanding of care and what I'm trying to do.

> I like to think the caring part underlies the whole process of your supervision. You're trying to make a relationship which is positive. It's an ideal of course but that's what 'caring about' means to me.

Similarly, elaborations on control, as suggested by those already quoted, frequently lapsed into self-conscious rationalisations of why the officer felt he/she should control probationers, rather than specifying why and in what way they were actually aiming to control them:

> I think officers often tend to sort of shy away from the controlling aspects, it's one of the less attractive parts of our job, it goes against the grain of self-determination. But personally I feel that it's often by controlling that we show clients we are caring - by saying no when they're being irresponsible - that's why I think the controlling aspect of our job should be important.

As an ethical raison d'etre the concepts therefore offer a convenient shorthand, encapsulating the social work standards and ideals of, inter alia, self-determination and obligations to others. In this light their persistence seems understandable. Nevertheless, prescribing what one ought to do is a conceptually different exercise to describing what one is actually doing. So again forceful grounds are established for replacing the concepts; replacement not in the sense of their outright rejection - for in normative terms they have clearly not outlived their usefulness - but instead replacement in the sense of relocating the concepts to a more appropriate analytic space i.e. the designation of social work values rather than supervisory aims.

An Alternative Typology of Aims

From her ethnographic study of probation practice, Axon concluded that the formulation of a typology of supervisory aims was doomed to failure because:

> different aims can be described depending on the worker's perspective and the contingencies of any given situation. (1977 p. 149)

Given the varied assortment of elaborations generated by the Berkshire sample it is tempting to agree with Axon but, on closer inspection, the data suggests that she may have mistaken the tendency to personalise supervisory aims for evidence of relativism. This observation is more than hair-splitting in that whereas the former provides for the existence of differences, the latter asserts that they are so extensive as not to be amenable to a coherent and manageable system of classification. Although differences could be identified in the elaborations, the diffuseness noted applied more to the concepts of care and control than aims per se and was not found to be so extensive as to mean that the elaborations were beyond the possibility of being classified in an alternative way. While there was ample evidence of the officers and probationers personalising their explanations of supervisory aims in relation to their perspectives and situations, this process, from scrutinising both groups' accounts, seemed to be facilitated for them by reference to either or both of two overarching aims. These in turn were based upon any one or a combination of four recurring objectives.

The first of these overarching aims was support which Folkard, in his typology of probation treatment derived from his study of officers' aims, defined as follows:

> anything which is said or done to help the offender solve or mitigate his personal or social problems. (1966 p. 16)

In the present study the identification of support as a supervisory aim arose from the frequent references made to 'counselling' and 'assisting' objectives. The reader can recall from the section before how the officers and probationers, although not always using the terms counselling and assisting, nonetheless described their understanding of supervisory objectives as entailing those elements constitutive of them. For example we can recollect the officer who spoke of reducing the probationers' painful pressures by either changing the way they thought about them i.e. counselling, or trying to take the pressure away i.e. assisting, and the probationers who described the purpose of their supervision as either 'having someone to confide in' and 'being given guidelines' i.e. counselling, or someone to give them 'help with difficulties like paying in fines' and 'help with reading trouble and finding a job in the papers' i.e. assisting. To this extent the traditional description of supervisory aims as consisting of advising and assisting (if not befriending [11]) might justifiably be reasserted in place of the more problematic concept of care. However, the nature of the other overarching aim prevents regarding them as a sufficiently comprehensive basis for classifying aims as has customarily been the case with official accounts (Jarvis 1980 p. 50). Thus the second overarching aim noted was <u>surveillance</u>. This was not only conceptually separate and distinct from <u>support</u> but also it could not be inferred from the traditional tripartite designation of supervisory aims. The formal application of the concept of surveillance to social work practice is fairly recent (Davies 1981), commentators and researchers alike preferring the concept of control. Folkard, for example, juxtaposes support with control in his typology of probation treatment. He defines the latter as,

> anything which is said or done to induce the offender to conform to socially acceptable standards of behaviour.
> (op. cit. p. 16)

This conceptual preference for control is unfortunate because, quite apart from the problems with the concept already recorded, typical definitions, like Folkard's, eclipse the presence of two distinguishable elements implied by the concept of surveillance and expressed by the officers and probationers as supervisory objectives; namely 'directing' <u>and</u> 'monitoring' behaviour. The reader can recall from the previous section how the officers and probationers, as well as referring to the control/surveillance idea of directing behaviour to induce conformity e.g. 'I instruct them to abide by the conditions of their orders', also frequently mentioned oversight and the objective of monitoring to see that they were doing so. This objective is insufficiently registered by the concept of control but would seem to be just as fundamental to the concept of surveillance as the idea of directing/superintending behaviour [12]. As one of the probationers put it, the monitoring objective could be regarded as a necessary precondition for the directing objective:

> To keep a check on you, to find out what you're doing to try and direct you into something different if it's illegal.

When the officers' and probationers' explanations of supervisory aims were grouped according to this alternative typology an interesting difference emerged between the two groups and is shown in Table 2.7.

Table 2.7
Officers' and probationers' explanations of supervisory aims

AIMS

	Support	Surveillance	Mixture
Officers	33	16	35
Probationers	20	33	31

x^2 = 9.328, d.f. 2, P < 0.01

Whereas pure surveillance was least popular among the officers it was the most popular aim with the probationers and suggested a prima facie case for the presence of diametrically opposed perspectives. However, although this difference proved statistically significant, close inspection of the accounts revealed the polarisation to be more apparent than evident. When individual pairs of officers' and probationers' comments were examined to confirm this trend, just under half of the sample, specifica#ly 47.6%, related identical aims with only fifteen cases or 17.9% having polarised views about the purpose of their supervision i.e. eleven where officers described the aims in support terms while the probationers concerned regarded them in surveillance terms and vice versa in four other instances. The differences found with the remainder of the cases were much less marked and consisted of one party seeing supervisory aims as either pure support or pure surveillance and the other a combination of the two. Again then, as with explaining offences, there was little empirical evidence to substantiate the assumption of some commentators that officers and probationers usually hold diametrically opposed perceptions of the purpose of supervision (Walker and Beaumont 1981).

The presence of support and surveillance as overarching aims of supervision - realised through the medium of counselling, assisting, directing and monitoring objectives - is hardly surprising given the justice and welfare roots of the Probation Service (King 1969). The Probation Rules, for example, place both a welfare oriented duty on officers in their supervision to advise and assist, and a justice oriented responsibility to,

> keep in close touch with a probationer, meet him frequently, and, unless there is good reason for not doing so, visit his residence from time to time and require him to report to him at stated intervals. (P.R. 1965 r. 35)

What was surprising however was first, the selectivity of the officers and the probationers in citing one or a combination of the apparently justice and welfare rooted objectives, and second, the link between both groups' justice and welfare orientations registered in their explanation of offences and the sort of supervisory aims that were perceived. Instead of those justice oriented toward offences seeing supervisory aims in surveillance terms and the welfare oriented in support terms, the justice and welfare orientations were applied to all four objectives. The Table below clearly demonstrates this.

Table 2.8
Officers' and probationers' aims by type of offence orientation

	OFFICERS' ORIENTATION		PROBATIONERS' ORIENTATION	
AIMS	Justice	Welfare	Justice	Welfare
Support	14	19	11	9
Surveillance	8	8	19	14
Mixture	17	18	16	15
	39	45	46	38

$x^2 = 0.356$, d.f. 2, N.S. $x^2 = 0.232$, d.f. 2, N.S.

Accordingly, rather than a division of welfare and support aims on the one hand and justice and surveillance aims on the other, it was necessary to extend the typology from four to eight major classes; the counselling, assisting, directing and monitoring objectives being either justice or welfare in orientation. Below, eight case examples are provided to illustrate the typology. It is however important to recognise that while these cases highlight a focus on one particular supervisory objective, many of the cases involved a combination or mixture of them e.g. counselling and assisting or counselling and monitoring.

Justice oriented support

In characterising the justice orientation to crime Tutt [13] points out that one of its defining features consists of the view that,

> if offending behaviour is a rational response to certain situations then it is reasonable to hold the individual responsible for his actions and accountable for those actions. (1982 p. 6)

When the officers and probationers explained their understanding of the supervisory aims in support terms this type of justice orientation was recognised by the emphasis placed upon the responsibilities for which the probation was liable and/or civil rights to which he/she was entitled.

Case example 1: justice oriented counselling

A thirty-four year old male was prosecuted for defrauding D.H.S.S. because he claimed not to have received a giro payment when he had and accepted an additional emergency payment from them. He had wanted the extra money so that he could buy a present for his ex-wife, with whom he was having an affair, without it interfering with his responsibilities to his common-law wife. The situation was complicated by the fact that his common-law wife was recently pregnant by him. The officer's aims were:

> To try and help him face up to his responsibilities and hopefully through talking with him about his domestic situation make him aware of his position as a husband and a father. He has to sort out whether he wants to stay with his common-law wife or return to his ex-wife and not selfishly go from one to the other as the whim takes him. I felt we also needed to look at his responsibility to the unborn child and whether he wanted to be around for the birth and afterwards which I very much doubted if he went on trying to fiddle D.H.S.S. to bail himself out domestically.

Case example 2: justice oriented assisting

An eighteen year old convicted of burglary, with several previous offences of dishonesty, explained how he saw the aim of supervision as being practical and related to his probation officer getting him what he was entitled to:

> It's to go and see them if you've got any problems. Like I didn't like going in the dole office. They keep you waiting

and treat you like shit. He said I had a right to me dole money so why didn't I make an appointment to see them. I said it was alright for him to make an appointment for me, so he did, and I just went in there myself after that.

Welfare oriented support

In differentiating the justice from the welfare approach, Tutt notes of the latter that it,

> adheres to the medical model of operation, going through stages of assessment (diagnosis) and treatment of the individual. This leads to a stress on assessing... problems and the development of individual treatment plans many of which focus on behaviour not shown to be directly related to offending. (ibid. p. 7)

Precisely the same kind of welfare orientation to the counselling and assisting objectives can be noted in the following two case examples.

Case example 3: welfare oriented counselling

A twenty year old male was prosecuted for possession of class A drugs. In the court report the officer emphasised 'his need to mature through a counselling relationship outside the family', going on to explain in the interview that the drugtaking was symptomatic of various 'problems in living' he was having:

> At the start of the order I asked him to tell me what were the things that caused him problems. One of the things he gets rather fed up about was that he was adopted. Secondly he feels differently from his friends - this might be a combination of both the adoption and the fact that he's starting to bald, he's going bald at a fairly early age. He drinks a lot, he's very susceptible to group pressure and finally I wanted to try and link in some coherent way his offending which was drugtaking with why he felt he wanted to or needed to. It transpired that he does get very low, gets terribly lethargic, feels as if there is just no point in going on. He's not clinically depressed but he has problems in living and my aim was to ask him what they were so that we could discuss together how we could go about doing something about them.

Case example 4: welfare oriented assisting

A twenty year old female was convicted of shoplifting for the second time and in the case file's Initial Assessment the officer had written that she saw the purpose of supervision as being, 'to help --- come to grips with the practical problems that overwhelm her'. During the interview the officer explained:

> She's an unmarried mother with two children who are both presenting problems for her. She has a little boy who is backward and a girl who is five months old and very ill in hospital and she lives in a one room basement flat. She's not very bright and frankly can't cope with the officials she

has to deal with. My aim was and has been to help her with getting rehoused and the practical problems with --- in hospital and visiting and trying to get her money for fares and liaising with the other people concerned like the hospital social worker, the housing department and the education department about her son. There are a lot of welfare problems which I have tended to concentrate on rather than the criminal aspect but hopefully the one will sort the other out.

Justice oriented surveillance

Those officers and probationers who, from a justice oriented perspective, explained the purpose of their supervision in surveillance terms, tended to emphasise the insisting upon and/or checking up that the probationers were fulfilling their legal obligations.

Case example 5: justice oriented directing

This officer's comments about a nineteen year old prosecuted for deception are typical:

> In my Part B Summaries I've used phrases like 'Too shrewd', 'Too clever by half', 'Too clever for his own good' and I feel sometimes that in interviews he's at least one step ahead of me and that in fact he's directing the situation ... So I've felt it's been important to catch him out and try and show him where he's going wrong by insisting upon him keeping to some agreed arrangement which in the first instance means keeping to his contract with the court to abide by the conditions of his probation order.

Case example 6: justice oriented monitoring

A sixteen year old shoplifter perceived his supervision as a form of tracking [14] whereby the risk of him reoffending was held in check by the knowledge that his activities and movements were being systematically monitored and at any time he could be required to account for them:

> P.: It's just to keep a sort of discreet eye on us, basically to keep tabs on us. I'm usually asked what I've been doing and what a certain thing was like. What I've been up to in my own time, you know, 'Have I been down the shops?' as well as at work.
>
> L.S.: What's the point of that?
>
> P.: It's to see that I'm not breaking the law, which is ok.

Welfare oriented surveillance

At first sight the idea that surveillance aims could be welfare oriented might seem to be a contradiction in terms, the latter having no conceptual link to and therefore operational truck with the former. However this would be to deny the existence of a wide range of counselling styles, of which, 'empathetic responding' may be seen at one pole and 'challenging' at the other. In the challenging style the accent is not on being a good listener and then responding with understanding, but on 'focusing on discrepancies in thought, feelings and actions' (Nelson-Jones 1983 p. 111) and therefore entails directing the probationer - albeit from a welfare orientation. It would also deny that the process of assessment described above by Tutt requires as a precondition intimate knowledge, and therefore monitoring, of the individual's personal circumstances so as to identify the factors contributing to the problem or problems. The following two case examples illustrate both points and conclude this alternative typology suggested by the respondent's elaborations on their understanding of supervisory aims.

Case example 7: welfare oriented directing

A nineteen year old gambler who had stolen from his employers to pay off his debts explained how the officer had been very directive with him about not covering up his problems:

> P.: I've had a gambling problem and once I lost some money and I was going to go and borrow and you know cover up and he said 'No, come clean'. And I did and it's a helluva lot better than what would have happened if I had gone on covering it up from my parents like I had in the past.
>
> L.S.: Is that what you see the purpose of your supervision as being?
>
> P.: Yea, I was once also made redundant from my job through having been there less time than anyone else and I didn't tell anybody. My P.O., who I always give my work's number to, phoned up with an appointment change and found out. I wasn't going to tell anyone until I'd got another job but he found out as I say and when I came to see him on the Monday he confronted me with it. He's always been an advocate of coming clean and not covering up.

Case example 8: welfare oriented monitoring

Monitoring the causes rather than the potential commission of further offences was the focus in some cases. In the Initial Assessment of this case the officer wrote:

> There have been no previous court appearances. --- is on supervision for an offence of theft by finding (a piece of jewellery). This is largely because there are serious problems at school. --- invariably arrives late, he feels he is picked on, he is definitely under achieving and he can be insolent towards some staff.

In the interview the officer explained her monitoring objectives:

> There was a specific problem, the school, and my intention

was to try and monitor the situation, to liaise with the school and to try and find out what was bugging him and making him behave in this very anti-social way at school.

In reviewing the characteristics of both groups to assess whether any of them were associated with and possibly influential in prompting particular supervisory aims to be chosen, only one association was found. Among the probationers, those with no previous convictions were much less likely to specify supervisory aims in pure surveillance terms, whereas the reverse was true for those with previous convictions.

Table 2.9
Probationers' criminal history by the aims they mentioned

CRIMINAL HISTORY	AIMS		
	Support	Surveillance	Mixture
Low	12	11	19
Medium/High*	8	22	12
	20	33	31

$x^2 = 6.046$, d.f. 2, $P < 0.05$

* It was necessary to combine the medium and high groups because of the small number of high cases.

The reason for this distribution, and possibly why collectively more of the probationers than the officers gave pure surveillance aims, appeared to relate to these probationers' previous experiences of the criminal justice system. These experiences tended to colour, not necessarily negatively, their views about the purpose of supervision: specifically that community supervision, like the larger system of which it is a part, is primarily concerned with surveillance and not support objectives. For example, one probationer with ten previous convictions described his probation order as 'like being in open prison', going on to explain how he saw the purpose as being to direct and monitor his behaviour in the community. For him this was more effective than 'lazing about twenty-four hours a day inside':

> It's harder to stay out here like with temptation you know, and with somebody pumpin' it into your head all the time, you know, it's there with you all the time. Whenever I go and see him he says 'Are you keeping out of trouble, what've you been up to, where've you been? Don't let temptation walk in your way, you're strong enough to say no, you're big enough to say no, so just say it'!

There was no such association among the officers nor with any other of the probationers' characteristics or, for that matter, the characteristics of the officers themselves. For example, none of the officers were narrowly committed to pure support or pure surveillance aims, the particular configuration of objectives depending on the case under review. As with their explanation of offences, instead of taking particular aims to all of the cases indiscriminately, they tended to personalise them so as to match what they perceived to be the particular needs of the case. For the officers to do this and deal coherently with what Axon terms 'the contingencies of any given situation', the existence of justice <u>and</u> welfare oriented types of support and surveillance appear to have been vital in providing a structure whereby this flexibility of approach could be accomplished without degenerating into relativism. Furthermore, the eightfold repertoire of aims also seemed to enable them in any one case to avoid the potential inconsistency of having to chop and change orientations because the particular objective selected belonged to one as distinct from the other of the orientations.

In addition to their operational utility for officers, it can also be provisionally argued that the concepts of support and surveillance developed here constitute a credible paradigmatic shift (Kuhn 1970) for understanding supervisory aims. Thus descriptively, if linked with the justice and welfare perspectives, these concepts provide a helpful means of classifying the variable nature of supervisory objectives. Similarly, when theorised in conjunction with the idea of personalisation, they create an analytic framework for making more precise and consistent sense of supervision than by previous commentators and researchers.

Supervisory aims are not therefore unclassifiable nor, when defined in terms of support and surveillance, prone to the kinds of problems identified with the concepts of care and control. This is not however to say that support and surveillance were free from problems, and this introduces a further shift in understanding prompted by them concerning a new dilemma for those doing supervision.

A New Dilemma

The double bind dilemma of supervision, because of the incompatibility between care and control, disappears with the rejection of these concepts; but could those replacing them also contain antithetical objectives? The cases were carefully examined to assess this possibility, but no evidence could be found for the existence of incompatibility. In the cases involving a mixture of aims, no support-surveillance conflict was indicated between either counselling and directing, assisting and monitoring, or any other configuration of mixed aims. As gradually became clear, an important reason for this absence of conflict at the level of explaining the purpose of supervision was the justice and welfare orientations to support and surveillance providing for a greater degree of cohesion between these two overarching aims than has hitherto been formally recognised. However, in the process of reaching this conclusion two fresh problems were discovered, both of which stem from a discrepancy between the rhetoric and the reality of aiming to exercise support and surveillance.

The support discrepancy

Support as an aim, whether approached from a justice or welfare perspective, attaches great importance to the probationer, so to speak, owning the problem and agreeing to the counselling and assisting thought appropriate to its resolution. Indeed the concept of the <u>contract</u>, which may be regarded as the cornerstone of either justice or welfare oriented support, depends on the participation of the probationer/client. As Reid and Epstein have argued:

> The major function of the contract is to ensure that the practitioner and client have a shared understanding of the purposes and content of treatment. The contract is formed at the beginning of service and, unless both parties agree to changing it, serves to guide the course of service... Most important, use of contracts with the unmotivated or uncertain client provides some assurance that he will not be treated 'behind his back' for conditions that have not been made clear to him. (Quoted in Davies 1981 p. 70)

As far as the beginning of statutory supervision is concerned, evidence from this research indicates that many probationers were either bewildered by or felt powerless to participate in the process of forming a contract. For example, just under a third of the probationers (27N) reported being so bewildered at court that they could not recall either being questioned about their understanding of juvenile supervision or their willingness to consent to adult probation. Neither the age of the probationer nor the absence or presence of previous court contact were associated with this bewilderment i.e. bewilderment being associated with a lack of sufficient life or court experience, and was fairly evenly spread on both counts [15]. The following comments were typical:

> I never had a clue what was going on and when I was told I had supervision I didn't even know what that was about.

> P.: I had no idea what probation was all about.

> L.S.: Weren't you supposed to agree to being placed on probation?

> P.: I don't know, no idea, I was in a daze in court. I can't remember them saying anything like that at all.

For a further fifteen of the adult probationers, bewilderment was less of a problem than a sense of powerlessness. Although all of them knew that their consent was necessary, none felt they were being invited to make a real decision, being more of a case of Hobson's Choice. As one of the probationer's put it:

> You accept it to keep your freedom. What's the alternative? If you say no they're not going to be too pleased. They're going to send you down aren't they.

The problem of bewilderment at court and the problematic nature of electing to submit to supervision is well documented (Carlen 1976, Walker and Beaumont 1981), but only four of the officers voiced concern about these discrepancies even though they present a serious problem for the aim of exercising support. Moreover, the commonly expressed solution of anticipating bewilderment and powerlessness at the social enquiry report stage i.e. by discussing both courtroom procedure and their proposed recommendation, must be judged against the fact that over a third of the probationers (29N) - including those reported on by the four officers aware of the problem - could not recall either a social enquiry report being undertaken or what the recommendation was!

The surveillance discrepancy

As Bochel (1976) has shown, the probation order has throughout its history been an alternative to punishment not an alternative punishment; a point more recently affirmed in law by Lord Bridge in the Cullen -v- Rogers ruling referred to in Chapter 1. The risk of aiming to exercise surveillance degenerating into punishment has however been regarded as a supervisory hazard for many years. Nearly two decades ago, for example, King observed:

> To the offender the probation order may appear as a punishment in itself: he is obliged to keep in touch, to receive visits, he has the feeling that the order is hanging over him throughout its duration. Even though such requirements and restrictions are imposed with the intention of helping rather than punishing, they can make probation far more exacting that a fine, which can be paid and forgotten.
> (1969 p. 9)

Although King stresses the helping as opposed to the punishing intent of this surveillance - a view shared by all the officers without exception - just over a third of the probationers (28N) appeared to miss the point, perceiving the surveillance aims of their supervision mainly or partly in a punitive way. For six the surveillance was 'mostly' punitive, for five 'fifty-fifty', and for seventeen 'partly' punitive. The most frequently reported punitive feature was having to report to the officer and the financial and personal inconvenience this entailed:

P.: Coming up here on the bus, having to spend money on bus fares and wasting your own time, I mean, you might make plans because you've forgotten about the probation and then you realise and all the plans are damaged. It's a punishment in that way.

L.S.: Does your probation officer say you have to come because it's a punishment?

P.: No, he says it's to make me a better appointment keeper, which it has, and I tend to get there on time which I didn't use to before.

Reviewing the characteristics of these probationers, their officers and the orientations of both, revealed no significant associations. Instead the reason for the discrepancy between the particular officers' and their probationers' perception of the aim of exercising surveillance seemed to revolve around the failure of either the officer to sufficiently spell out, or the probationer to accept, the justice or welfare oriented reason for the surveillance. As King pointed out, a punitive element to supervision may make it 'more publicly acceptable' but at a cost of undermining the whole point of supervision. In the context of the present research the evidence suggests that those officers who fail to dispel the punitive perception of surveillance aims held by a substantial proportion of probationers, do so at a <u>potential</u> cost of undermining the whole point of the surveillance.

In this chapter an attempt has been made to map the officers' and probationers' explanations of crime and the supervisory responses which follow them. Notwithstanding the limitations of the sample from which the findings have been obtained, and the consequent danger of over-generalising, the data would seem to suggest that officers do not keep to a uniform explanation but make personal sense of each case depending on its particular circumstances. However, as with the probationers, the process of making sense was neither free-floating nor unclassifiable. Rather we have seen how the domain assumptions of the justice and welfare perspectives constitute a resource, not only for an explanation of crime - mediated by the psychological and sociological axes - but also for interpreting the subsequent supervisory aims. In turn these were shown to be more accurately and adequately classified in terms of support and surveillance than care and control. The discrepancies found between the rhetoric and the reality of support and surveillance provides both a cautionary note to conclude with and a link with the four chapters to follow. In each of these chapters an attempt will be made to assess the link between the idea of probation practice and the practice of the probation idea.

Notes

[1] Supervisory styles may have changed since the Morison Committee reported but nevertheless retain a commitment to the principle of relying on 'the individual's own account of himself'. See for example Walker and Beaumont (op. cit.).
[2] Gouldner, from whom the concept of domain assumptions derives, defines them as 'the things attributed to all members of a domain: in part they are shaped by the thinker's world hypotheses and, in turn, they shape his deliberately wrought theories' (1977 p. 31).
[3] Although Parsloe identifies a third approach i.e. the community approach, she does acknowledge that it is 'harder to describe because it is only slowly gaining ground and can barely be seen in the operation of the criminal justice system' (op. cit. p. 73). Moreover, the description she does provide seems to be more in line with an extension of, rather than departure from, the welfare perspective i.e. 'those who are poor who come from ghetto areas, who have a poor education, are unemployed and, in America, are black...' (ibid.).
[4] See for example Limont's exposition of the justice perspective (1976).
[5] See their note 24.
[6] A minor problem was encountered with the opportunistic type of explanation where, in a small number of cases (8N), the clause 'what everybody else does' was rejected; but even here the basic orientation and focus was still accepted vis. 'decided to take a chance and was unlucky getting caught doing what everybody else would do given the opportunity'.

[7]   Interestingly, this was more of an issue for officers than probationers; 7N of the former complaining against only 1N of the latter.

[7]   For example, comparing the characteristics of the biased officers, the likeliest association seemed to be of younger officers choosing welfare explanations while older officers preferred justice ones. However, the Fisher test put the level of statistical significance well outside the 5% limit i.e. P = 28.6%; a result obtained in all the other comparisons made, both between the welfare and justice biased group, and the biased with the unbiased group.

[8]   If one bears in mind the welfare rationale of the Children and Young Persons Act 1969 which provides a statutory basis for supervising juveniles, the prevalence of such an assumption is hardly surprising. See Thorpe et al (1980) for a discussion of the welfare orientation of successive Childrens' Acts.

[9]   Interestingly, the possibility that the younger the probationer the more likely a welfare explanation would be given in preference to a justice one did not prove to be the case for either the officers or the probationers. When the adults were grouped according to 17-20, 21-29 and 30+ age divisions, the welfare biased distribution was fairly evenly spread.

[10] Broadly speaking five competing and incommensurable 'paradigms' (Kuhn 1970) of care and control can be identified. Compare and contrast, for example, the pure-care model where the officer's role is theorised as being to serve the needs of the offender (Harris 1977 and 1980) with the pure-control model where it is formulated as being to serve the requirements of the court (Limont 1976 and Griffiths 1982). In addition to these two mutually exclusive accounts there are two further inclusive accounts i.e. the controlling-care and the caring-control models. Here the emphasis is on either facilitative control to serve the needs of the offender by concentrating on the requirements of the court (Hunt 1964); or facilitative care to serve the requirements of the court by concentrating on the needs of the offender (Winnicott 1962 and Raynor 1978 pp. 421-422). More recently a speculative control-plus-care model has been formulated which seeks to combine offender needs and court requirements by operating conditional freedom with unconditional help (Bryant et al 1978 and Bottoms & McWilliams 1979). Although these models have advanced a series of conflicting claims none have been verified empirically. In short they all share a polemical rather than practical status.

[11] As Timms has argued, the concept of befriending belongs to the history of social work and is 'not easily applied' to present day social work; not least because it is a concept - one might say like care and control - 'about which it is easy to disagree' (1964 p. 80). Winch, for example, considers the notion of friendship to be debased when applied to the context of social work because it obscures the 'divided loyalty, not to say double dealing' structurally determined by the social worker's first duty to the policy of the employing agency (1976 p. 123). Moreover, from a purely empirical standpoint it is worth noting that only one of the officers (who incidentally used the word interchangeably with assisting) and

none of the probationers referred to the concept directly or ideas suggestive of it. For these reasons the concept of befriending, as far as designating supervisory aims was concerned, was dispensed with.

[12] See for example the definition of surveillance contained in the Shorter Oxford English Dictionary (1978 p. 2203).

[13] Although Tutt's remarks are confined to juveniles, a review of the literature suggests they could equally be applied to adults. See for example Parsloe (1976).

[14] The term _tracking_ derives from a scheme initially piloted in Leeds and consists of monitoring the whereabouts, involvements and associations of offenders, through requiring them to report to a tracker in the community three times a day (Sharon 1984).

[15] The bewildered probationers consisted of eleven juveniles and sixteen adults, and fourteen with previous convictions and thirteen with none.

3 Association

The Theme of Association

Since the Probation of Offenders' Act (1907) contact between the officer and the probationer has been the linchpin of probation practice, simply because without it supervision would be impossible. As an early handbook of probation stated:

> Unless close contact is maintained, not only with the probationer but with his family it would be impossible adequately to supervise treatment. (Le Mesurier 1935 p. 128)

Indeed three decades later the Morison Committee, in its review of the probation service, pointed out that it was precisely the need for 'continuing attention' which distinguished the probation order from other non-custodial disposals like the fine or conditional discharge (op. cit. p. 4). However, in spite of its importance, studies of the association between officers and probationers have been largely piecemeal and descriptive: concentrating on one particular aspect of it, or examining the subject generally in passing as part of a broader project. Although useful clues about the frequency, location and composition of officer-probationer contact can be inferred from the material available, it nevertheless lacks sufficient detail for a comprehensive analysis. Consequently, whether certain types of supervisory aims involve certain types of association, or particular kinds of officers and probationers tend to engage in particular kinds of contact, remains uncertain. In this chapter therefore the findings obtained from previous studies will be linked with those obtained from the present sample with a view to clarifying how often, where, and with whom officers and probationers meet, as well as the supervisory aims, assessments, and characteristics of those involved in these different types of association.

Frequency of Contact [1]

From piecing together the results of previous research it appears that the frequency of contact between officers and probationers is not uniform throughout the period of supervision. Instead it is generally greatest during the first quarter, after which it declines progressively. The move from high to medium to low contact seems to commence after the first month, shifting from roughly weekly interviews to around fortnightly meetings; the subsequent level of contact gradually decreasing to monthly visits at the end of the order [2]. This pattern applies to both adult and juvenile probationers and seems to be the result of a blend of justice and welfare oriented reasoning. On the one hand, the Probation Rules state that the intervals the officer should meet the probationer,

> shall be determined amongst other circumstances by his behaviour and progress and regard shall be had to the importance of frequent meetings during the early part of the probation period. (P.R. 1965 r. 35[2])

with the underlying message to officers to judge and reward progress by diminishing the frequency of contact. On the other hand, Monger's (op. cit.) identification of the first, central and terminal phases of supervision, described in Chapter 1, would appear to correspond from a welfare oriented standpoint to the different levels of contact recorded by researchers, i.e. focusing on understanding, problem solving and working through client dependence [3].

Consequently, whether approached from a justice or welfare perspective a rationale exists for this high then medium then low frequency of contact. Perhaps not surprisingly therefore a similar pattern - at least so far as the first and central phases were concerned - was also found for the majority of the Berkshire sample when their earliest and latest quarters of contact were tabulated.

As the Table below clearly demonstrates, during the initial quarter over two thirds of the cases had a high frequency of meetings i.e. once a week or more, but by the central quarter the proportion had fallen dramatically with a commensurate rise in the number having a medium level of contact i.e. fortnightly or once every three weeks. As one of the officers explained, this pattern of high to medium contact was more than a coincidence, and it is interesting to note how her remarks mirror the guidelines of the Probation Rules:

> I would normally start off by seeing people once a week and that's just a pattern. And then when I am satisfied with their progress it switches to fortnightly, and that can take anything from a month to six months to get to that stage. I think that's very common practice.

For both of the phases reviewed there were however exceptions to the general pattern of contact. For example, in the initial phase

Table 3.1:
The average frequency of interviews for the initial and central phase quarters *

CONTACT		INITIAL PHASE QUARTER		CENTRAL PHASE QUARTER	
		N	%	N	%
High	(twice a week	5	5.9	0	0
	(once a week	54	64.3	27	32.1
Medium	(once a fortnight	23	27.4	29	34.5
	(once every 3 weeks	1	1.2	13	15.5
Low	(once a month	1	1.2	14	16.7
	(over once a month	0	0	1	1.2
		84	100	84	100

* These figures are based on Part C file entries made by the officers after each interview, having been cross-checked with the officers' and probationers' accounts to ensure their validity. Because the case duration at the research interview differed between probationers, the latest quarters referred to also varied. Nevertheless, the steps that were taken to standardise this data (see Chapter 1) were thought to be sufficient to justify situating each case within the central phase of supervision and facilitate a comparison of the cases' initial and central phase experiences. For convenience of presentation the two periods reviewed are referred to hereafter as the initial and central quarters.

the norm was for weekly contact but 6% (5N) of the cases were seen more often and 30% (29N) were seen less. Similarly, during the central phase although 50% had, as expected, a medium level of contact, the other 50% were seen at either a higher or lower frequency. Because the duration of the cases in the central phase varied, the possibility that the high or low levels of contact simply reflected the newness or oldness of the orders was considered but not found to be significant. When the average duration of the high contact cases was compared with the average for the low contact cases they were very similar i.e. Mean = 9.5, S.D. 2.6 compared with Mean = 9.7, S.D. 2.2. This departure from the expected pattern therefore introduced the alternative possibilities that either supervisory aims or particular sample attributes were influential in determining the level of contact. Regarding aims there was the suspicion, engendered by some of the officers' comments, that pure support cases were being seen proportionately more in the initial phase and less often in the central phase than pure surveillance cases because of a commitment to a crisis intervention as distinct from crisis prevention approach. Whereas in the former contact is 'immediate, focused and time limited' (Butrym op. cit. p. 32) based on providing intense psychological and practical support for the purpose of alleviating the crisis i.e. in this context the conditions underpinning the current offence, crisis prevention entails a more routine pattern to avoid future crises i.e. further offences. One of the officers, for example, in implementing her aim to counsel and assist a probationer with massive debts which had culminated in defrauding D.H.S.S. went as far as stating that much of her work in this and other similar cases was undertaken at the pre-sentence stage:

> I do a lot of work, casework, at the S.E.R. stage and however busy I am I still seem to do that because in a sense, in the long term that's time saved. The more you can do at that stage, a very vulnerable stage, the better, because it can sometimes be very productive and can cut down, as I see it, the need for quite a lengthy order and contact where you have to take it slowly.

Alternatively, another officer indicated his view of the appropriateness of maintaining regular contact for the purpose of directing the probationer toward 'living by certain rules' and in the process avoid a tenth court appearance:

> --- was in a state when I first met him. He had no discipline, he wasn't able to discipline himself and he had no rules to live by. So regular reporting has reintroduced him to living by certain rules and imposing internal discipline.

To test whether these individual instances reflected a collective tendency, the cases were grouped according to the officers' supervisory aims by the frequency of contact.

Table 3.2
Officers' aims and the frequency of contact with probationers

AIMS*	\multicolumn{2}{c}{Initial Quarter}		\multicolumn{3}{c}{Central Quarter}	
	High	Medium/Low**	High	Medium	Low
Support	22	11	7	18	8
Surveillance	11	5	3	10	3
Mixture	26	9	17	14	4
	59	25	27	42	15

$x^2 = 0.496$, d.f. 2, N.S. $x^2 = 7.965$, d.f. 4, N.S.

* It was decided to concentrate on officers' aims because, as will be discussed more fully later, they determined the frequency of contact in the vast majority of cases.

** These two levels of contact were combined because the number of expected frequencies falling below 5N exceeded the 20% rule was arranged in a 3 x 3 table (Siegel op. cit.).

As can be seen above, no statistically significant association could be demonstrated for either quarter. This is not, however, to say that the officers' supervisory aims had little influence in determining the level of contact. From scrutinising the officers' accounts it gradually became clear that both high and low levels of contact could be and were in fact linked with support or surveillance aims, depending on the case under review [4]. To illustrate this, four examples are provided - two of support and two of surveillance- where the probationers were seen either above or below the expected rate for both quarters.

High-contact support

A nineteen year old female, placed on probation following theft from her employers, was seen twice weekly during the initial quarter and weekly by the central quarter. In the file her offence was described as a 'panic response to debts, accommodation difficulties and accumulated hurt from a disturbed and unsettled background', and the officer's plan was to 'offer a consistent stable fulcrum of support'. In the fieldwork interview he explained:

> She is a particularly fragile, vulnerable person. I have actually given her the option of always having free access to me. It's not something I do with every client but with somebody whose accommodation and mental state is in a state of flux, I've felt there's been a need to be available more often than usual and therefore I have been.

High-contact surveillance

A fifteen year old male, prosecuted for a series of thefts from cars while truanting, had been given a supervision order with the suggestion from the magistrates that daily reporting be instituted. The officer considered this impracticable and settled instead for twice weekly contact at the start and weekly contact thereafter. In the Initial Assessment written by the officer the link between her surveillance aims and the high frequency of contact was made explicit:

> I believe he is seriously delinquent and shall be surprised if a supervision order is sufficient to contain him. I plan to take a consistently black and white line with him and initially to require frequent reporting, at least twice weekly, to reinforce school discipline.

Low-contact support

A nineteen year old male received a probation order following the theft of a cheque book and attempting to forge a cheque to pay off his mounting debts. At the time of the offence he had been unemployed and homeless. However, by the time of the court appearance he had found temporary accommodation and his financial crisis was over. The officer therefore decided that a low level of contact was appropriate i.e. fortnightly initially and monthly subsequently. In the file the officer wrote:

He has found himself a job and his next task will be to find more permanent accommodation of which he seems capable. Therefore I have arranged our interviews at fortnightly intervals and have explained that the topics for conversation or examination will be pinpointed as and when the problems arise.

Low-contact surveillance

A twenty-one year old male narrowly escaped a further custodial sentence following his umpteenth burglary because he was able to satisfy the officer and the court that he had finally realised that 'crime doesn't pay'. The officer therefore considered giving him a 'fairly loose rein', seeing him fortnightly at the start but quickly reducing the rate of contact to just over monthly intervals:

> When I served the probation order we spent some time talking about the reporting arrangements. He was determined to go straight and break the established pattern of recidivism. I was fairly confident that he would take the reporting seriously and it seemed appropriate to acknowledge his resolve by keeping him on a fairly loose rein monitoring the situation fortnightly at first.

Although a relationship between the officers' particular supervisory aims and the particular frequencies of contact they determined could be identified, no such connection could be noted with respect to any of the officers' social characteristics and how frequently they meet with the probationers. For the central quarter all of the officers had high, medium and low levels of contact and although this was not so for the initial quarter, where three had a uniformly high level of contact with their probationers, the proportion was too small to be statistically significant. Thus in spite of the fact that these three officers were all male with three or more years length of service, the Fisher Exact Test results were well outside the 5% level of significance (P = 9.615% and 15.385% respectively). Similarly, none of the probationers' characteristics were significantly associated with any particular frequency of contact for either quarter. At both times the characteristics were fairly evenly distributed as the chi squared values obtained and shown below in Table 3.3 suggest. At first sight this negative finding may appear surprising because it seems to contradict a number of commonly held assumptions. For example that juveniles, because of their immaturity or waywardness, would have a less loose rein than adults. Similarly that serious offenders or those with several previous convictions, because of the implied risk to the community, would be seen more frequently than petty or first offenders. However it would have been surprising if this had been so because, as with the officers' aims, the high, medium or low levels of contact found with each of the probationers' characteristics depended on the particular circumstances of the case. Thus, having personalised their supervisory aims, the officers carried this through to the personalisation of the reporting arrangements - albeit within the broad parameters of reducing the level of contact between the start and finish - matching the frequency of meeting to the needs perceived or presented by the probationers, rather than their social characteristics per se.

Table 3.3
The probationers' characteristics and the frequency of contact during both quarters

CHARACTERISTICS*	INITIAL QUARTER	CENTRAL QUARTER
Age	$x^2 = 0.0^42$, d.f. 1, N.S.	$x^2 = 2.372$, d.f. 2, N.S.
Gender	$X^2 = 1.193$, d.f. 1, N.S.	$x^2 = 0.265$, d.f. 2, N.S.
Class	$x^2 = 0.0^34$, d.f. 1, N.S.	$x^2 = 1.772$, d.f. 2, N.S.
Offence Gravity	$x^2 = 1.826$, d.f. 2, N.S.	$x^2 = 4.767$, d.f. 4, N.S.
Criminal history	$x^2 = 0.565$, d.f. 2, N.S.	$x^2 = 2.865$, d.f. 4, N.S.

* The classification of the characteristics is the same here as in Tables 2.3 and 2.4 e.g. age was based on a comparison of the frequency of contact for adults and juveniles.

The relationship between the idea and the practice of probation in the reporting context can be assessed not only in terms of the number of contacts made, but also with regard to who decided them. Two questions follow from this focus. First, did officers with a directing objective decide the frequency of contact alone? Second, did those with purely supportive aims either share the decision with or leave it entirely to the probationer, thereby reinstating the conditions for an authentic contract and in the process redress the <u>support discrepancy</u> noted in the previous chapter? For both the officers and the probationers the answers to these questions were an unequivocal yes to the first and no to the second. During the two quarters the decision was nearly always or mostly made by the officer, rarely or sometimes made together, and never by the probationer alone. For the initial quarter the officers and probationers estimated that the former decided in 97.6% (the officers' estimate) or 86.2% (the probationers' estimate) of the cases, with the remainder being shared decisions. Similarly, during the central quarter most of the decisions were described as having been decided by the officer i.e. 78.3% from their own estimates and 63.3% from the probationers', while again the rest were reported as shared decisions.

The absence of a support-choice/surveillance no-choice pattern does not however preclude the possibility of reference to support or surveillance reasons for this one-sided style of decision making. King, for example, identifies two reasons for the officer deciding alone and it is interesting to note how the first echoes support reasoning and the second the logic of surveillance:

> Many probationers are initially unaware of their need for help, neither conscious of having problems nor of being problems and they have no expectation that people in authority can be helpful or understanding. Secondly, the element of compulsion brings probation officer and probationer face to face with the whole problem of authority which may be fundamental to the latter's conflict with society. (op. cit. p. 96)

For King therefore the officer deciding the reporting arrangements can either be a means to an end i.e. support focus, or an end in itself i.e. surveillance focus, and the same reasons were often given by the officers:

> My deciding when to meet enables regular contact to be set up which will establish a relationship, a working relationship to develop, where any of the problems which led to the probation or supervision order being made can be looked at and dealt with.
>
> I don't give clients the option of deciding, at least at the outset. (L.S.: Why is that?) Because for some it serves as a useful reminder of their obligation and responsibilities. I really do believe there is some merit in that discipline in itself. Whatever else happens, whatever else the probation officer may say to you, whatever else he may involve you in, the actual discipline of having to keep appointments and come to a particular place at a particular time have beneficial effects on some people, not everybody, but on some people.

The decision to decide <u>for</u> instead of <u>with</u> the probationer and its danger of degenerating into a questionable paternalism [5] was, however, tempered by a common concern of the officers to be as flexible as possible in exercising their power to compel the probationers to report to them:

> Whenever you've asked me about any of my cases you say 'Who decides?' and I say 'I decide'. I give the same answer every time but there's more to me deciding the frequency than saying 'Right, you've been put on supervision, come and see me or else!' I say 'Well I'd like to see you once a week at the beginning of the order and we'll see how things go and then we'll make it less often' and then I say 'See you next Monday if that'll suit you?'. So there's a certain amount of choice. I make it clear I don't want to interfere with jobs or school or anything like that. I can see them in the evening and so on, so they've got that much choice. But deciding how often they see me, yes, at the start that's my decision but towards the end of the order it can work out fifty-fifty. I say, 'Look here we're near the end of the order so we can meet less often, what would suit you?'.

This kind of approach, as well as accounting for the difference between the number of officers and probationers estimating how many of the reporting arrangements were the result of a shared rather than one-sided decision, probably explains the fairly high level of satisfaction among the probationers with the frequency of contact decided. For the initial quarter 66% and for the central quarter 58% said they would have seen the officer for either the same amount or more often, if it had been possible, with no discernible bias in terms of their officers' supervisory aims, or their own social characteristics. Nevertheless a sizeable minority were dissatisfied, though the reasons for this seem less to do with the quantity of contact than its quality. For those expressing a preference for meeting less often there appeared to be a loss of interest in the purpose of their supervision, while those never wishing to meet rejected the supervisory aims perceived outright and therefore the usefulness of any contact. With the former, inconvenience was often presented as the reason for meeting less, underpinned by a feeling that contact had become superficial and mechanical:

> It's alright if I'm going into town to do some shopping, you know, I can sort of pop into the office and pass the time but otherwise like last Thursday, I thought 'Oh, I've got to traipse into town', you know, sit there for a quarter of an hour and talk over the same things like last time. It was alright in the beginning, we had a lot of things to sort out, like between me and my husband, but we seem to be talking over the same things and I don't think we're getting anywhere now.

Others however dismissed the value of any contact whatsoever, either for support or surveillance purposes:

> Seeing my probation officer is a waste of time. She hasn't helped me at all. At one point she said she'd help me find a job but I found me own job and I didn't need a probation officer for that. I got a ticking off from the court, I didn't need the probation officer to do that for me either.

Dissatisfaction can of course lead to the probationer failing to report and because non-reporting constitutes such a fundamental challenge to probation practice the officers and probationers were invited to share their experiences and thoughts about infrequency of contact.

Infrequency of Contact

In spite of its primacy in potentially undermining the supervisory process, probationers missing appointments has attracted little research interest or commentary. The standard commentaries of Parsloe (1967), King (1969) and Monger (1972) for example, only mention the subject in passing as one of the grounds for <u>breaching</u> the probationer i.e. returning to court to be sanctioned for failing to comply with the terms of the order, without any discussion of how often probationers might be expected to miss appointments; why this was; and at what stage breaching would be appropriate. Lawson (1978) does however note from his study of officers' use of the power to breach probationers that non-reporting was the second commonest reason for breaching, although persistent non-reporting which usually resulted in breach proceedings tended to be exceptional. By contrast he observes that 'the occasional failure to keep an appointment is an everyday occurrence' (p. 11) and has little effect on the supervisory process. In the Berkshire sample a similar pattern was discovered but a number of points emerged regarding the extent, reasons for and consequences of non-reporting which warrant more than a passing comment.

Firstly, based on a comparison of infrequency levels for the initial and central quarters, an association was noted between the prevalence of missing appointments and the duration of the orders.

As Table 3.4 below shows, the older the order the greater the number of missed appointments. Indeed when the data from the two periods was dichotomised into on the one hand, those cases missing under a third of the total appointments given, and on the other, those missing over a third, the result was statistically significant (x^2 = 9.764, d.f. 2, P < 0.01). Why was this? In a rare discussion of probationers missing appointments, Foren and Bailey (1968) advance two reasons for non-reporting which, although they consider applicable throughout the duration of the order, might conceivably become more prevalent as time goes on and therefore explain the different levels found for the two periods:

> There are some occasions when a client's failure to comply with the requirement to report indicates an attempt to test the limits _either_ of his permitted behaviour _or_ of the worker's concern for him (p. 101).

Table 3.4
The proportion of missed appointments for both quarters

PROPORTION*	INITIAL QUARTER		CENTRAL QUARTER	
	N	%	N	%
None	44	52.4	27	32.1
Low	31	36.9	35	41.7
Medium	7	8.3	16	19.1
High	2	2.4	6	7.1
	84	100.00	84	100.00

* Low = under a third, medium = between a third and two-thirds, and high = over two-thirds of the appointments given.

It is interesting to note how each of these reasons could be taken as a direct reaction to the officers' support or surveillance aims and provide a hypothetical link between the idea of probation practice and problems attending its implementation. For example, in line with the case illustrations given by Foren and Bailey, some probationers might regret disclosing personal information to the officer and subsequently decide to miss further counselling sessions; while others could react to being directed what to do by not reporting. The possibility of both support and surveillance cases missing appointments was certainly upheld in that for both periods those keeping and missing appointments were evenly distributed according to supervisory aims. However, from examining the officers' and probationers' accounts, although similar explanations were given by both groups for both periods, they were broader than the testing of limits suggested by Foren and Bailey. Furthermore, there appeared to be a close connection between the amount of non-reporting registered and the reasons for this.

For those cases missing under a third of the total appointments given during either period, the absences were usually regarded by both parties as being for legitimate reasons. In the main these referred to the individual having to work late, being kept on at school, illness or getting the reporting day wrong; especially when the sequence of reporting changed or conflicted with a public holiday. These 'accidents of fate', as one officer put it, were seen as one-off instances having little effect upon and therefore significance for the supervisory process much like Lawson's everyday occurrence of the occasional failure to report. By contrast, medium and high levels of non-reporting were considered significant not only because the number of missed appointments was much greater, but also because the reasons for them represented a challenge either by default or design to the officers' supervisory plans. Whereas the medium level of absenteeism was often associated with an apathetic attitude towards supervision i.e. a challenge by default, the high level of non-reporting invariably signified rebelliousness i.e. a challenge by design. For the apathetic probationers the pattern was to miss between a third and two-thirds of the appointments given either because they were so indifferent to supervision that they forgot when their appointments were or, even if they knew, preferred to do something else instead if an opportunity happened to arise. This was irrespective of the officers' aims. In some instances, as the remarks of the following officer-probationer pair illustrate, the probationers were uninterested in the support on offer:

> Well the usual reason given is he simply forgot. He forgets or sometimes there's been a conflict with some other more attractive thing like going fishing or going on an outing somewhere. He'd rather do that than sit and talk to me about himself.

> You see I like playing football and when I get in a game I lose all sense of time and forget all about where I've got to go.

In other cases the probationers were unconcerned about the officers' surveillance aims and appeared to suffer from a form of selective amnesia:

> The reasons are usually forgetfulness or illness: (laughing) he has these memory lapses round about the time he's supposed to report.

> I just couldn't be bothered to come. I was ill once but to be honest it's dead boring. He asks me the same questions every time, 'What have I been up to, am I staying away from trouble?': I'm alright, I'm not a bad lad. I just come in to keep the peace. You know, when I remember to or he reminds me.

The doubling in size of this apathetic group of probationers between the initial and central quarters seems to have resulted from, to borrow a concept from Weber (1964), the routinisation of supervision's charisma; where an apathetic sense of going through the motions had replaced the memory and acuity of the court appearance and/or the reasons for it. The following exchanges were typical:

L.S.: How come you didn't miss any appointments at the start?

P.: It seems more serious your first time on probation, you think it's really serious, you must go and you must see her otherwise you'll get in all this deep trouble and that. But as it sort of drags out towards the end, you know, you become less bothered, 'cause you know you've only got three or four months left on probation and they can't do much really. It matters more at the start 'cause, you know, they're trying to sort of write reports about you and everything and it doesn't go down very well with the court does it.

P.: Either I've forgotten or something else was happening.

L.S.: Do you think it mattered that you've missed these appointments recently?

P.: No not really, not now, it would have mattered early on.

L.S.: Why was that?

P.: 'cause I was going through a bit of a funny period then, you know, a bit of a suspect stage where your mind's a bit confused, you know, about what to do.

Among the rebellious group it was supervision that was suspect, either right from the outset or later on; again irrespective of the officers' aims. For these particular probationers the trend was to miss over two-thirds of the appointments given. The reasons approximated to Foren and Bailey's testing of limits in as much as some of the probationers rejected the offer of support, while others objected to the exercise of surveillance. In one case, for example, missing appointments had been a problem from the outset because the probationer had consistently refused to participate in the counselling planned by the officer. Repeated attempts had been made to establish regular contact 'to get some communication going' and the officer was at pains to point out that,

> although he _had_ to come, what I was trying to do was something other than just enforcing the legal requirements.

However the probationer was not persuaded:

> It's personal reasons why I haven't come down and seen him. Mainly because things were going sort of bad and there didn't seem - I knew what he was going to say before I came down here. I didn't really want to face anybody, least of all a probation officer. (L.S.: Why least of all a probation officer?) There was nothing he could do by my going down there and talking. It makes things worse. I've lost everything, my wife, my daughter. Words aren't going to bring them back are they?

In another case dissatisfaction only appears to have arisen later in the order but once present a vicious circle seemed to follow where the officer's reaction to the non-reporting only reinforced the reasons for it in the first place i.e. objection to the officers's surveillance aims:

> I missed one and then he sent me a letter and I thought 'Sod it I'm not bothering anymore', 'cause I thought I'd been on it long enough. And then I rung and said 'Oh I'm ill' and I told him lies. Then he sent me another letter and I missed it again and I said I was working away when I wasn't and he found out. He checked up on me which I thought was a bit much. So he sent me a recorded delivery threatening to take me back to court and have me prosecuted for the original offences for breaking the probation order, so I thought I'd better come in (laughing) and cover myself better next time.

As this quote illustrates, a number of ruses were employed by the rebellious group to avoid reporting. In addition to concocting legitimate-seeming excuses such as those tried unsuccessfully above, two further ploys appeared popular. These entailed telephoning either just before or just after an appointment to make another one, or failing this, cutting the interview short through arriving late or a variety of verbal and non-verbal stratagems:

> If I phone up and say I can't make it that day, or I phone up after I've missed the appointment and say 'I'm sorry I didn't come, I was held up somewhere' he just gives me another appointment. He doesn't mind if I phone but if I just don't turn up and don't give any sort of notice he gets annoyed. First of all I didn't bother ringing and every time I came in I felt a bit uncomfortable, 'Why didn't you come?' you know, 'Why didn't you let me know?'. So I thought it's better phoning up really because then you more or less get away with it.

> If I want to get away quick I sit there looking at the floor letting her do all the talking 'cause she soon gets fed up with it and lets me go. Or I chat to her and look at my watch now and again and say 'Oh, my bus is going in five minutes', and she'll get the hint and let me go.

How then did the officers manage non-reporting and the reasons for it, especially the challenging absences presented by the apathetic and rebellious probationers? From the scant research and commentary available there appear to be only two options open to the officer: either letting the missed appointment pass as an expected commonplace or breaching the probationer. However, the evidence from the Berkshire sample suggested a more complex <u>tariff</u> was operated by the officers consisting of four distinguishable responses expressed along a continuum of severity. These ranged from tolerating to reproaching to threatening to breaching and were closely related to the proportion of appointments missed.

<u>Tolerating</u>

This response followed appointments rarely missed and these absences were always designated by the officers and probationers as being for legitimate reasons. In many instances, because of the regular pattern of contact hitherto, the officers simply ignored the absence and expected the probationer to report the next time as usual. Alternatively, a telephone call was made or letter sent giving a fresh appointment, delivered in a passive style suggesting that the equilibrium of the supervisory process had not been disturbed. The following letter illustrates this:

> Dear ---
>
> I was sorry you missed your appointment last Thursday. I hope nothing is wrong. Can you come and see me next Thursday, 20 November at the usual time.
>
> I look forward to seeing you then.

Reproaching

The reproaching response was usually applied to the apathetic probationers and involved a more assertive though still relatively mild reaction from the officers. This consisted of reminding the probationer of the missed appointment(s) and, depending on the officer's particular supervisory aims, that this was against the rules of probation/supervision i.e. surveillance, a barrier to being helped i.e. support, or both i.e. a mixture. The general tone of the communication, whether by letter, telephone call, or, in some cases special home visit, was 'try not to let it happen again':

> Dear ---
>
> We had an arrangement for you to call on me here yesterday (Tuesday) evening but you did not arrive once again.
>
> As you know it is an important condition of your probation order that you keep in contact in accordance with the arrangements made. When you don't keep appointments and don't let me know why, then you are breaking the conditions of your order.
>
> I hope you are getting on alright. If you aren't I can only help you if you come and see me.
>
> Could you please come and see me next Thursday evening 5th August at 5.30pm.

Threatening

The threatening response was reserved mainly for the rebellious probationers - though a few of the apathetic group were also threatened - and entailed listing the number of missed appointments, repeating the legal significance and consequences of persistent non-reporting and issuing an ultimatum to report 'or else':

> Dear ---
>
> I wrote to you on 28th October asking you to report to me here on 30th October. You did not keep the appointment and it was the second in a row that you have missed.
>
> You agreed to the making of the probation order and to keep its conditions. If you do not come when I ask you to, then the arrangement is not working as it should do and we shall have to go back to court and ask for your offence to be dealt with in some other way.
>
> Please call on me at the office this Thursday evening 6th November at 6.30pm <u>without fail</u>. If you do not keep this appointment, then I shall ask the court to summon you for breach of probation.

If the communication was by letter it was sent recorded delivery, and direct face to face confrontation, usually via a home visit, was preferred to telephoning.

<u>Breaching</u>

This is self explanatory and in fact occurred with two of the adult probationers, both of whom had a record of persistently high non-reporting and open hostility to being on probation.

The existence of this tariff was noteworthy for three reasons. First, because there were no national or local guidelines to explain its presence. Second, because from an organisational standpoint, it was shared by all of the officers for all of the non-reporters regardless of their supervisory aims or the probationers' particular social characteristics. Although, for example, the emphasis of the censure did vary according to the supervisory aims, all the censured probationers nevertheless progressed up the tariff from the tolerant response upwards. Invariably it was in direct proportion to the amount of non-reporting registered with only a small degree of discretion being exercised between the implementation of the various responses. Unexpectedly therefore officers did not <u>personalise</u> their reaction to the missed appointments to anything like the extent they had done with arranging them in the first place. A possible explanation of this collectively shared behaviour could be that it constituted an 'occupational survival' strategy (Satyamurti 1981) to manage the probationers' resistance to both the officers' aims and their statutory responsibility for ensuring compliance with this fundamental feature of the order. As one officer typically observed:

> If they're not reporting they're not getting any benefit out of supervision and they're not meeting the requirements of their order. You can't ignore it. You're not doing your job, you're colluding with the client and not helping him solve whatever problems he's got and if the management find out it's panic stations, you know it's not the sort of thing the case committee* want to hear.

* A committee, mainly composed of magistrates, who review the work of probation officers.

The absence of a differentiated response to the probationers in terms of their social characteristics was, however, less surprising for two reasons. First, because no discernible differences were found between the characteristics of either the three groups of non-reporters or those of the non-reporters taken as a whole and compared with those of the good reporters i.e. non-reporting was not a problem specific to a particular type of probationer which therefore attracted a particular kind of response. Second, because of the organisational and operational constraints experienced by officers that were mentioned in the quotation above. In this light the general application of the tariff to manage a general problem can perhaps be appreciated.

Shifting from an organisational standpoint to an interactionist perspective, the operation of this tariff was also noteworthy because it appeared to resemble a form of gamesmanship between the officer and the probationer similar to two of the social games described by Scott (1968); namely the relationship and the exploitation games. According to Scott:

> In relationship games, the participants seek to create, maintain, attenuate or terminate personal relationships. In exploitation games, the participants seek to maximise their position of power and influence vis a vis one another.
> (p. 159)

Thus for the co-operative probationers who missed few or no appointments there was no manipulation and counter-manipulation. The contact between the officer and probationer instead appeared to exemplify what Walker and Beaumont, utilising Gramsci's theory of hegemony, have described as the 'consent securing role of probation work' (1981 p. 162) i.e. the relationship game. In these, the majority of cases, the officer's professional expertise and/or statutory authority was seen as legitimate by the probationer and the creation and eventual termination of a relationship the means to achieving the reformative aims, whether support or surveillance in focus. However, when nearly as many if not more appointments were missed than kept the relationship game was undermined. Depending on the extent of and reasons for the non-reporting, this resulted in a series of graduated ploys and counter-ploys between the officers and the apathetic or rebellious probationers whereby each pair attempted to maximise their respective influence and power, typical of the exploitation game. For Walker and Beaumont, this micro-interactional process, if theorised from a macro-structural perspective, signifies 'the threat of coercion (which) underpins the probation officer/client relationship'. To a certain extent the experience of the reporting-wise rebellious group would appear to confirm this. Thus, although as shown before tariff experience sometimes enabled them to successfully avoid appointments, their influence was eventually overridden by the power of the officer through threat or actual breach. However, the power was not entirely one-sided because, whereas in one of the breaches the order continued and the reporting improved i.e. the officer having his way, in the other the probationer adamantly refused the help offered by the officer and the order was discharged and replaced with a conditional discharge i.e. the probationer having his way [6].

The sample from which these findings about infrequency of contact have been obtained although rather small for the purposes of generalising from, may nevertheless provide some useful hypotheses concerning the existence, operation and consequences of this non-reporting tariff for researchers to examine in future.

Location of Contact

The interplay between the idea and the practice of probation in the context of association can also be examined in relation to where, as distinct from how often, contact takes place. Twenty years ago Folkard (1966) reported that contact was predominantly office-based with only a small proportion of meetings taking place in the probationer's home. Subsequent research concerning both adult and juvenile probationers suggests there has been little change in this practice [7]. In discussing the location of contact Monger (op. cit.) while acknowledging the advantages of home visits in forging an informative relationship with members of the probationer's family, nevertheless proposes two main reasons why the office is preferred by officers as the principal venue. Firstly, it avoids the distractions inherent in a home visit and encourages the probationer's mind to be focused on the meeting with the officer. Secondly, the officer is 'in control of the situation' and therefore able to:

> further his understanding, demonstrate his wish to help, his ability to control, his willingness to allow freedom, his approval of the client, his capacity to absolve guilt, his sense of humour, or whatever the prevalent need may be
> (p. 108).

Monger excludes none of these possibilities from the home visit but argues they can be more effectively achieved in the office, where the officer does not have to fight a losing battle with the television, or interruptions from inquisitive neighbours, pets or small children.

More recently, however, commentators and researchers have questioned the appropriateness of this reliance on office contact. Bottoms and McWilliams (op. cit.) claim for example that to make statutory supervision more meaningful and therefore effective, officers need to engage much more with probationers outside the office. They quote Morris and Beverly's findings on parolees as being the typical experience of all categories of offenders supervised by officers:

> Most parolees thought that the understanding probation officers had of them as people, and of their life styles, was very limited ... visits to the probation officer were regarded as something 'apart' from all other aspects of their lives... the relationship was not seen to impinge upon their other social roles - as husbands, fathers, workers and so forth. (p. 169)

Similarly Parker et al (1981), from their study of juvenile supervision, question in passing the professional rhetoric which legitimises office-based contact. They suggest that meeting in the office is probably no more than an administrative expedient, being 'tremendously convenient and efficient for the officer'. Yet, they observe, notwithstanding the danger of an over concentration on the juvenile as being the problem, this is contrary to the family-centred spirit of the 1969 Act, where seeing the juvenile's problems and offending in their broader familial context is paramount:

> The family-centred approach is more likely to pick up a range of issues arguably related to offending but certainly related to a youngster's needs or interest. Our own interview visits, for instance, led us into the midst of major family rifts, rows and crises which were simply unknown to the probation officer supervising the juvenile. (p. 142)

On the face of it there appeared to be little acknowledgement of these concerns by Berkshire officers because, as Table 3.5 below shows, for both the initial and central quarters the office remained the principal venue in the vast majority of cases.

Table 3.5
The principal meeting arrangements for the initial and central quarters

VENUE	INITIAL QUARTER		CENTRAL QUARTER	
	N	%	N	%
Office	70	83.30	75	89.3
Probationer's home	5	5.95	3	3.5
Office and probationer's home	5	5.95	4	4.8
Elsewhere	4*	4.8	2*	2.4
	84	100.00	84	100.00

* During the initial quarter two cases were receiving in-patient psychiatric treatment and were seen in hospital but by the central quarter they had been discharged and were seen at the office. All the other elsewhere cases were seen at local church or town halls to offset the travelling distance for these probationers.

Although during both phases nearly half of the principally office-based probationers were seen once or twice at home, sometimes together with one-off visits to their school, work, or neutral places like local clubs or pubs, environmental contact never assumed the prominence proposed by its advocates. In the main non-office contact seemed confined to a literal interpretation of the Probation Rules that probationers should be seen in their environment 'from time to time' (P.R. 1965 r. 34, 35 and 36). Responsibility for the predominance of office contact appeared to rest mostly with the officers who, as with the decision when to meet, were usually regarded by both parties as the one who decided the arrangement [8]. Administrative expedience was rarely mentioned or indicated and their reasons for preferring office contact often corresponded with those cited by Monger. Collectively, however, the officers did seem to hold the view that certain supervisory aims were better served by office contact. As an icebreaker to their counselling objectives, for example, officers sometimes met with the probationers in local clubs, pubs, or in one case, the officer's own home; but invariably the office was preferred as the 'better environment for discussion':

> There are home visits from a voluntary associate. You see I've got someone else doing the practical work. I saw my role as different (pause) basically to talk with --- about the situation calmly and quietly without being interrupted every five minutes and losing the thread; and the only way to do that I felt was in the office. It's a better environment for discussion.

It was not however that support was undertaken in the office and surveillance outside. Officers frequently mentioned the advantages of office contact and directing probationers to fulfil their obligations through, among other things, the example of having to report to the office. In this connection it is significant to note that the officers were unsympathetic to those commentators critical of the location of probation offices near to court and police buildings (Harris 1977) because of the deterrent value associated with such proximity. As one officer typically observed when reflecting on an eighteen year old prosecuted for a series of car thefts:

> He's on probation for quite serious offences and I think that the fact that he has an obligation to the court is something that he doesn't take terribly seriously and I think he has to be reminded of it by having to report to the office. Especially as he has to pass by the police station and court house to get here.

Environmental contact was nevertheless valued by officers but usually it was for the purposes of either assisting or monitoring the probationers. Regarding the former, one officer, much to the chagrin of her colleagues who felt she ran a serious risk of compromising either herself or their own concern to retain their privacy, invited probationers to her own home to do odd jobs and earn some money for themselves. Less controversially and more frequently, officers concentrated on seeing probationers in their homes when practical work was a primary focus. In the following example an officer was concerned that the young mother's domestic problems might lead to further drinking and, in turn, further trouble through drink:

> She's a single parent and was having a lot of difficulty getting her children to go to bed when told so I did several home visits with a child guidance co-worker. We used a star chart system and that seems to have been tremendously successful plus allowing mum and the children to talk about each other in front of each other in the security of their home.

Home visits and other environmental contacts were considered useful not only in assisting probationers with their problems but in finding out what their problems might be in the first place. Sometimes this was welfare oriented and geared to monitoring family dynamics e.g. in the home, or peer group interaction e.g. at a local club or pub; at others it was justice oriented and geared to ensuring compliance with the terms of the order. In the example below the officer relied on home contact to ensure that the probationer was living an honest if not industrious life:

> At one time he deliberately deceived me, letting me think he was still in work when he wasn't. I would never have found out had it not been for the home visit. He's quite a liar but his mother tells me the truth so we were able to have it out.

Ironically, when the probationers were invited to comment on the location of contact, a much greater proportion were satisfied with the existing arrangements than advocates of environmental contact might have led one to expect. The results suggest that, at least so far as adult probation and juvenile supervision are concerned, it is the commentators rather than the practitioners who appear out of touch with the probationers' needs or wishes. For example, during the initial quarter only a third preferred a different set of arrangements (29N), with a similar proportion for the central quarter (33N). Indeed in only three cases for the former phase and three for the latter were unconventional venues like local clubs, pubs or the officer's home mentioned. Expressed another way, when the preferences were tabulated only twelve probationers during the initial quarter and sixteen by the central quarter were dissatisfied with any form of office contact. Furthermore, thirteen others for each of the quarters said they would have preferred to be seen in the office exclusively!

When the reasons for those preferring to be seen at home instead of the office were examined a common denominator was found relating to the duration of the order. During the initial quarter the newness of the order was frequently referred to as the reason for disliking office contact. Many of these probationers were concerned about employers seeing them enter the probation office, while others were apprehensive about the relationship between the probation service and the police because of the two buildings being so close together. These concerns relate to the problem of stigma and are considered more fully in Chapter 6 but for present purposes one probationer's remarks provide a useful summary of these fears:

> 'cause of the police station right next door, I felt that they were together somehow, being so close. I felt that they were, I don't know, hand in hand with the police somehow. I felt that what I said to him was going back to the police but he's informed me that it's not. (L.S.: Why don't you mind coming to the office now?) I think I had a complex before that everyone was seeing me walking down the police station and I've got used to it now and I don't mind anymore. It doesn't bother me.

As with this probationer, most overcame their initial concerns but dislike of office contact due to the newness of the order was later replaced with a dissatisfaction due to the order's oldness. The problem of the probationers losing interest or becoming disenchanted with their supervision has already been noted in previous sections and was reflected here in a preference for the least inconvenient place to meet, namely, the probationer's home. Interestingly, this preference was especially marked among the adult female probationers whose initial commitment to probation was clearly on the wane due to their pressing domestic responsibilities.

Table 3.6
Venue preferences during the central quarter according to gender

GENDER	VENUE	
	Home	Other
Males	6	18
Females	7	2
	13	20

P = 0.913% i.e. within the 5% significance limit of the Fisher Exact Test.

One probationer who was happy to visit the office during the early quarter for example, no longer felt willing or able to keep up the commitment:

> I've been going through a difficult time lately (laughs). I'm always going through a difficult time and being seen here in my house would be much easier for me, you know, not having to make arrangements for the children with my neighbour; having to rush back and cook their tea, you know, that sort of thing.

For those preferring to be seen in the office exclusively the age of the order was much less important than the age of the probationer. During both phases the vast majority of these probationers were living at home with their parents and felt either spied on when visited at home or, even more frequently, inhibited to speak there. The following comments were typical:

> I feel a bit on edge when I'm at home, I'm frightened to say what I feel; but when you come to the office you can say what you feel or think.

> I can't usually talk freely in front of my parents, they interrupt me or laugh at what I say.

Not surprisingly many were juveniles; a finding which raises serious doubts about the viability of the family-centred approach, described earlier, because this runs directly counter to current thinking and the emphasis on the 'family nexus' (Webb and Harris 1984). The result was tested statistically to see if it could have arisen by chance but, as the table below indicates, this was certainly not the case.

Table 3.7
Venue preferences during both quarters according to age

AGE	VENUE	
	Office	Other
Adults	7	25
Juveniles	19	11
	26	36

$x^2 = 10.864$, d.f. 1, $P < 0.001$

All the officers, unlike many commentators, recognised this problem and for this reason seem usually to have rationed the amount of home contact with juveniles and probationers living with their parents unless the home environment was a primary focus of their supervisory work. One of the officers explained, regarding juveniles, that while it was 'right to refer back to the home situation' to clarify everyone's roles and dispel any fantasies,

> that particular age group usually have a totally separate existence away from home, if you follow my drift - they do not identify as very close with their parents at that age and if they've actually got their own probation officer they prefer to keep them to themselves, keep them free from their home. If you want them to act like adults you have to treat them like adults not as mum and dad's naughty boy.

Instead of estranging the officers from these probationers, meeting in the office therefore actually served to bring them closer together. Although this unexpected finding partly contradicts some recent criticism of office-based contact, the rationing of home contacts with juveniles, when seen in context, appears as both an understandable basis for their effective supervision as well as an illustration of the complex interplay between the idea and the practice of doing supervision. A final aspect of association that was considered, and which also produced some surprising results, related to the composition of contact and the equally if not more controversial debate between traditional one-to-one casework and groupwork.

The Composition of Contact

The composition of contact may be regarded as the final cornerstone of probation practice alongside the frequency, infrequency, and location of contact. It refers not to how often or where but with whom contact takes place. Although, according to Monger (op. cit. p. 186), it hardly needs a sociologist to point out to a probation officer how important groups are in a probationer's life experience, sociologists researching the composition of contact during the sixties and seventies consistently indicated how individual casework was preferred to groupwork (Barr 1966, Davies 1974). Davies for example found that, out of a sample of 463 young male probationers there were only two instances where groupwork was proposed. Moreover, in only one of these cases was the proposal that the probationer participate in a series of discussions with other probationers followed up (op. cit. p. 75)! To assess whether this type of situation had persisted into the eighties and, if so, the reasons for this, case records for the whole of the period of supervision were examined and the sample interviewed to elicit their views on the advantages and disadvantages of groupwork [9]. In addition, the oral and written material was also examined to see if the composition of contact preferred was connected in any way to the officers' supervisory aims.

Was it so, for example, that the four supervisory objectives were considered more effectively accomplished on an individual basis, contrary to Parsloe's apparently unheeded challenge to this view during the sixties?

> Many delinquents commit their offences in company with others and such behaviour is a group solution to problems common to the group. It thus seems reasonable to hope that changes in behaviour might be affected more easily by group methods than by individual treatment since such offenders have demonstrated their dependence upon group pressures and group approval. (1967 p. 46)

Unexpectedly, as Table 3.8 below shows, the evidence immediately signalled the fact that officers' preference for office-based contact did not equate with a preference for undertaking individual casework e.g. only a quarter of the sample were seen exclusively alone.

Table 3.8
The extent of groupwork contact*

PROPORTION **	N	%
None	21	25
Low	36	42.9
Medium	12	14.3
High	15	17.8
	84	100.00

* This Table does not include information relating to Intermediate Treatment because none of the officers were directly involved in supervising the nine probationers on these schemes. Instead, it registers the proportion of contacts between the officer and probationer which, as part of the supervision plan, were shared with other probationers or relatives of the probationer - as distinct from contacts between the officer and probationer alone.

** Low = under a third, Medium = between a third and two-thirds, and High = over two-thirds of the total contacts made.

Furthermore few of the probationers involved in groups for only a low proportion of their supervisory contact were seen with others simply for the purpose of fulfilling what Davies has described as the officers' 'nominal role of maintaining contact' (op. cit. p. 25).

The commitment of the officers to broadening the composition of contact beyond the traditional one-to-one dyad was reflected in the diversity of groups noted. Family work was the most popular group activity, accounting for just over half of all the groupwork (33N), and involved seeing the probationers with their parents, spouse or children. The rest of the probationers were engaged in either task-centred/problem-focused groupwork involving like situated peers in issues relating to employment, social functioning and particular offences (9N), or co-defendants or friends also on supervision (4N). In just over a quarter of the cases (17N), probationers participated in a combination of these three main types of groups. However, whatever the type of groupwork, instead of constituting an alternative to individual treatment as Parsloe had argued, officers seemed to refer to utilise the two methods in conjunction with each other. Sometimes the group informed the major work undertaken in the individual sessions. At other times the position was reversed; but the two were invariably seen as complementary. The following officer illustrates this in relation to the marital work he was doing:

> I think the single sessions with --- are less rewarding, because I feel that if she has some dissatisfaction with the way things are going between her and her husband, there's not a lot of point in discussing them without him being there; though sometimes it's been helpful as a complement to the other kind of session because she's come out with more negative feeling about the way things are going, when he's not been there, and then I've fed that back in when he's been present again.

Therefore, depending on the reader's political perspective, the groupwork undertaken by the officers represented either a positive or negative extension of casework. In the former view it extends the possibility of 'seeing the whole of a client's life' (Monger op. cit.), while in the latter it perpetuates the tendency to individualise probationers' problems and engender privatised rather than collective solutions to public ills (Walker and Beaumont op. cit.). Either way officers and commentators were in agreement that groupwork could be undertaken for the purpose of accomplishing any one or a combination of the four supervisory objectives. For example, Monger's checklist of the advantages of groupwork (op. cit. p. 187), while not framed in the vocabulary of support and surveillance, is nonetheless suggestive of it. On the one hand there is groupwork's general value of enhancing self understanding and aiding communication i.e. support, and on the other, its facility for breaking down resistance to socially irresponsible behaviour and observing probationers interact in a natural setting i.e. surveillance. The officers also tended to frame their replies in these terms, although the most notable point to emerge was how no association could be found between particular aims being served by particular groups. Instead, the relationship between specific groups and the aims they were seen to serve depended on the particular circumstances of the case. Different groups could and did serve the same aims while in other instances the same group served different aims. For example, in the city team a sex offenders' group was run and two of the officers (who incidentally co-led the group) had arranged attendance for two of their probationers for quite different reasons. In the first case the aim was clearly supportive, yet in the second, support was overshadowed by a primary concern with surveillance:

> The purpose is to help him by being with other men who've had the same problems as him, and the same painful experiences as a result of the problems, so he doesn't feel on his own and a freak.

> I think the group is more productive than my individual sessions in the sense that other people will have felt the same pressures and desires that he feels and will have learnt the lesson that he needs to learn; namely that you have total control over your own actions, that it is ultimately up to you. And I mean that comes far stronger from someone who's actually learnt that lesson himself than from some probation officer preaching to you.

Given the diversity of groups noted and the variety of aims served, it is perhaps not surprising that the majority of the officers undertook some kind of group activity with the probationers and that no significant differences were found between the social characteristics of those probationers seen in groups and those who were not. In short, a stereotypical pro-groupwork officer seeing a uniform group of probationers could not be substantiated. In this respect the findings therefore depart from Barr's (op. cit.) observation that probation groupwork was usually practiced by male rather than female officers, with juveniles and young people as distinct from adults. However, bearing in mind that Barr's study was undertaken nearly twenty years before the fieldwork reported here, this discrepancy in findings is not particularly surprising. Perhaps it would have been more surprising if the present sample's supervisory styles had not differed from their colleagues of two decades ago.

An important and unexpected difference within the present sample was however discovered when the attitudes of the participating officers and probationers toward groupwork were compared; the latter tending to be less sympathetic than the former. The results are summarised in Table 3.9 below. While the officers might have expected to find the corporate management of a group of individuals technically difficult to accomplish (Monger op. cit.) and therefore prone to negative results, the greater concentration of negative responses from the probationers was unexpected. This is simply because it contradicts the basic assumption advanced by proponents of probation groupwork that probationers, apart from deriving benefit from the experience, would actually enjoy being seen with others rather than on their own. However, on closer inspection of the participants' accounts, group contact was found comparatively to be no more or less successful than individual contact. Instead the success or failure of either arrangement depended on the needs perceived by the person concerned. This finding was endorsed by the fact that, for both the officers and probationers, the distribution

Table 3.9
The attitude of participants toward groupwork

ATTITUDE

	Positive		Negative		Mixed		Total	
	N	%	N	%	N	%	N	%
Officers	27	42.9	13	20.6	23	36.5	63	100
Probationers	23	36.5	28	44.4	12	19.1	63	100

$x^2 = 9.274$, d.f. 2, $P < 0.01$

observed for particular types of groups approximated to the distribution of positive, negative and mixed feelings found generally. Accordingly the advantages and disadvantages of groupwork, from either the practitioners or recipients standpoint, would seem to be common to groupwork generally rather than particular types of groups. Elaborations on one or a combination of the four supervisory objectives represented the advantages and were more often perceived by the officers than the probationers. Alternatively, two main kinds of reasons were cited for the dissatisfaction and were more frequently registered by the probationers than the officers.

The first and most frequently mentioned reason constituted something of a paradox in that it referred to precisely the problem groupwork was supposed to overcome; namely the probationer's lack of confidence. This became evident from statements about feeling inhibited in a group and being unable to communicate with others. Some were able to overcome their inhibitions:

> There was a bit of a barrier at first, the first couple of weeks, but after a time, like in the social skills group - I mean I went in and felt a bit of a turd - but after a couple of weeks it was alright 'cause I could talk to the other blokes and I could talk to the probation officers and everything.

However this tended to be the exception not the rule and the comments of the juveniles, quoted in the previous section, who were unhappy about being seen at home with their parents because they felt inhibited, were more typical for all of the age groups seen with various others. Indeed of the twenty-one probationers not seen in groups, as many as nineteen of them felt negative about broadening the composition of their contact with the officer usually for this reason. As a twenty-five year old with paradoxical fluency put it:

> I would say it was 'cause I'm a shy person and I don't talk unless somebody asks me a question. I tend to sit back and listen. He has suggested me going to group lessons (social functioning group) but it wouldn't help me 'cause I'm very shy and couldn't talk. I get very nervous and tongue tied.

The second - less often cited - reason for dissatisfaction,

concerns the issue of confidentiality. Here an inability to communicate was superceded by an unwillingness. The issue of confidentiality is as old as probation groupwork literature and Barr (op. cit. pp. 57-58) provides a useful summary of its three distinguishable component problems. First, there is the problem of the officer disclosing privately obtained information about the individual to the group; second, the problem of the probationer divulging information which the officer feels obligated to report to some other person outside the group; and third, the problem of a group member sharing information about another member, again to an outsider. Interestingly, none of the officers or probationers mentioned the second problem but the first seemed especially acute in family work, while the third more usually arose with the other types of group.

The probationers' lack of confidence or concern about confidentiality, while forming the basis of an understanding of their resistance to or dissatisfaction with broadening the composition of contact, also raises the theme of interaction and provides an introduction to the next chapter where attention to the structure of supervision is followed by a focus on its substance. If links could be made between the idea and the practice of probation in relation to the theme of association, could the same be said for the theme of interaction?

Notes

[1] Originally it was planned to combine the frequency of contact with the duration of the interviews to produce a comprehensive picture of the extent of association between the officer and the probationer. However, it was necessary to abandon analysing interview lengths because over half of the case files failed to systematically record this information and many of the officers and probationers doubted their ability to recall the lengths accurately. Nevertheless, the comments on the lengths of interviews provided a useful supplement to those obtained for the number of interviews.

[2] The figures for adults are taken from the average number of contacts per month reported in Folkard et al (1976 p. 10) for controls and retrospective cases i.e. those probationers subject to ordinary rather than experimental probation practice, and from Giller and Morris (1978 p. 151) for juveniles.

[3] A similar perspective can be noted in King's summary of the casework process in probation: 'As a rule, the most intensive work, both in diagnosis and treatment tends to take place during the early part of the order. There are exceptions to this ... But with the majority contacts become less frequent during the latter part of the order, and the probation officer retires into a more passive role, watching the probationer's progress and giving support where necessary' (1969 p. 107).

[4] To a certain extent this finding replicates Folkard's reported in the interim evaluation of the IMPACT study i.e. 'more interviews were held in connection with high support/high control and fewer in connection with low support/low control' (1974 p. 5).

[5] See Kittrie (1972) for a general critique of the doctrine of parents patriae which holds that interference by the state with a person's liberty is justified if it is for his own good; and Harris (1980) for a discussion of the limitations of the family metaphor where the probation officer is cast in the role of a surrogate parent to the probationer child.

[6] Ironically both of these outcomes were regarded as Pyrrhic victories by the defeated parties: the probationer brought into line still resenting being on probation, and the officer in the other pair feeling the probationer had only succeeded in manipulating himself away from the help he needed. See Chapter 5 for a fuller discussion of breaching.

[7] In 1974, for example, the IMPACT study found that the control group of adult probationers had between 60% and 70% of their contact in the office, while Giller and Morris (1978) and Parker et al (1981) both reported that juvenile supervision was conducted usually in the office and only occasionally in the home.

[8] For example, probationers never decided alone and, although shared decision-making increased over time, the officers from either their own or the probationers' estimates retained the lion's share i.e. 90% (officers) or 84% (probationers) for the initial quarter and 82% or 75% for the central quarter.

[9] All of supervision was reviewed, rather than the initial and central quarters only, because the compositon of contact was found to be more variable than the frequency and location of contact; a significant proportion of contacts with others taking place outside the two periods.

4 Interaction

The Theme of Interaction

If association makes supervision possible what is the nature of the interaction which routinely accompanies it? This question is especially relevant to probation practice because of the importance attached by commentators since the Morison Committee not only in securing contact between the officer and probationer, but also to developing a relationship from it. Indeed as the Morison Committee observed:

> It is the appreciation of and concentration upon, the probationer's ability to benefit from a developing personal relationship with the probation officer that principally distinguishes probation supervision today from that of a quarter century ago. (1962 p. 25)

Although supervisory styles may have changed during the last quarter century, probation commentaries written from both mainstream and radical perspectives nevertheless still agree on the importance of the relationship and its dependence on the interaction underpinning it. Without systematic contact supervision may be impossible, but without systematic interaction the contact would be pointless (Day 1981, Kirwin 1985).

As Goffman (1967) once noted, the boundaries of social interaction have yet to be charted; but presently, few would dispute that they encompass a great deal of verbal and non-verbal material. Probation practice is no exception but three topics frequently referred to by social interaction theorists (Gahagan 1984) seemed particularly relevant to the focus of this research; namely conversation, comprehension and conflict. What, for example, do officers and probationers talk about when they meet? During these conversations do they understand each other, and, following on from this, how much if any disagreement is there between them? Furthermore, given the concern here to link the idea with the practice of probation, do any of these aspects of officer-probationer interaction vary significantly between different aims, officers or probationers? Although the answers to these and other questions posed in this chapter cannot pretend to represent a complete catalogue of probation interaction [1], they nonetheless attempt to build upon the scant research and largely speculative commentary which has addressed it since the Morison Report.

Conversation

In this section attention is focused on the verbal exchange between officers and probationers during their interviews with particular reference to the content and share each party estimated they contributed to the conversations [2]. The importance of this focus has been stated by Davies:

> No matter what the setting, no matter what the focus, the greater part of social work hinges on the nature and quality of relationships between workers and clients, and the basic tool in such relationships consists of verbal contributions by the worker and verbally expressed reactions by him to the client (1981 p. 47).

The content of conversations

What then are the topics of conversation in the probation setting and can any patterns be identified? In Table 4.1 the conversational material reported by both groups is listed.

Table 4.1
The top ten topics of conversation between officers and probationers

OFFICERS (N=251)		PROBATIONERS (N=210)	
Topic	%*	Topic	%
Family relationships	60.7	Family relationships	50
Work	53.6	Work	44.1
Leisure	44.1	Leisure	44.1
Personal problems	33.3	Personal problems	38.1
Marital relationships**	33.3	Marital relationships	22.6
Reconviction	21.4	Reconviction	16.7
Education	20.2	Education	15.5
Finance	16.7	Finance	9.5
Accommodation	13.1	Accommodation	6.0
Original offence	2.4	Original offence	3.6

* These percentages represent the percentage number of cases in the sample (84N) where these topics were mentioned e.g. for the officers there were 51 cases where family relationships were mentioned, hence 60.7%.
** Marital relationships include cohabitees.

Although the officers tended to cite the various topics more often than the probationers, the Table is nevertheless striking for the identical reference to and ranking of the major topics of conversation and indicates the general parity of perception of the two groups. Methodologically, this finding is a useful vindication of the rejection of the notion of the probationer as a judgmental dope, unable to volunteer information of equal credibility as that provided by the officer. More significantly however from the officers' standpoint, the Table goes some way toward empirically dispelling the disquiet expressed by some commentators concerning the class and cultural differences between officers and probationers; specifically that they are so wide as to estrange the two parties not only from deciding their priorities satisfactorily but from agreeing what they were when they talked about them (Walker and Beaumont 1981). The Table also demonstrates quite conclusively for both groups that conversations tended to be differentiated rather than uniform, consisting of between two and three major topics being discussed per pair (officers Mean = 3 and probationers Mean = 2.5). In this respect probation interaction appears to have more in common with the psychiatric than the legal interview i.e. the conversational material tending to be multi-faceted, ranging over a variety of topics relevant to the individual, rather than being focused on a single issue of concern (Cain 1979).

Although differentiated, certain topics of conversation were nevertheless more frequently mentioned than others. Moreover, the rank order here is particularly interesting because it replicates the findings from previous research undertaken with smaller samples, and suggests the presence of a conversational agenda routinely referred to by officers and probationers during their interaction. For example Davies' (1979) survey of adult probationers and Giller and Morris' (1978) sample of juvenile probationers both found that family relationships, leisure and work were the most popular topics, while past and future trouble with the law tended to be, as Giller and Morris put it, 'played down'. In the present study the relatively low position of offending in the conversational agenda may appear contradictory, given the commitment of a large proportion of the officers to partly or pure surveillance aims. However, from their accounts this seems to be more a reflection of the dynamic nature of probation interaction rather than a relegation by them of the importance of offending. Thus the majority expressed the view that discussion of the original offence was most appropriate during the social enquiry report stage and early phase of supervision, after which it was important to 'move on'. As one officer said, 'You can't go forwards by constantly looking backwards at the offence'. Similarly, discussion of the factors likely to precipitate a fresh offence seemed preferred by many to discussing further trouble per se; especially because of their concern that constant talk of reoffending would harm the relationship of trust they were trying to foster. This was a point by no means lost on some of the probationers:

> Well I think it would be wrong for any probation officer to keep doing that. It's just like by doing that to my mind you would be upsetting the person on probation all the time, not helping them. Just say I was a probation officer and you were the person on probation. If I say week after week to

you um 'Here Jim have you been breaking into Woolworths lately, have you, can you keep your fingers out of trouble?'; well if I said that to you practically every time I come and see you what would your attitude be to me? I know what your attitude would be. 'That miserable old bugger. I ain't gonna have much to do with you'. That'd be your attitude. But if I only approach it when you're first on probation and then forget the subject, then you'll find that the probation officer and the person on probation will work better together.

From the officers' perspective however, the decision about whether to regularly discuss further offences was not always quite so clear cut and a few, like the following officer, remained uncertain about the issue:

Is it important to be asking that question 'Well are you behaving yourself this week?', or is it important to avoid that, pretend that it doesn't exist as a notion? I think it's a very very difficult one. I suspect that the courts would expect that, but in terms of actually growing, maturing, getting it right, stopping them being delinquent, can you do it and avoid those sort of questions? Or are those questions vital to the process? I don't know.

The relationship between the officers' supervisory aims and the major topics of conversation was, as the remarks on offending illustrate, more complex than a simple matching of certain topics to certain aims subject to the exigencies of the case. Nevertheless, although in accordance with the complexity of the process no statistically significant association could be demonstrated overall between particular topics and aims, there were a number of discernible biases in this direction registered by both the officers and probationers. For example, from the officers' estimates twice as many support as surveillance cases discussed the probationers' personal life whereas the reverse was true for further trouble. Similarly, discussion of family relationships was dominated by proportionately more of the support than the surveillance group (73%:38%), while leisure featured as a topic for proportionately more of the latter than the former (63%:21%).

Not every topic was skewed in this way and employment was the most notable exception, being fairly evenly spread among both the pure and mixed aim clusters. Here though, as with all the other topics, another important bias was identified, this time transcending both the subject matter and the supervisory objectives involved. Whatever the topic or aims, conversations appeared to assume either a justice or welfare inflection indicative of officers carrying through and probationers detecting the perspectives initially used to make sense of the original offences. Support oriented conversations concerned with family relationships, for example, were often divided between either clarifying family obligations, 'I think the main things have been the rules that his parents set', or family dynamics, 'We talk about my dad a lot, if he's coming back or not and how I feel about it'. Similarly, many of the surveillance oriented discussions about leisure were pitched at either checking recreational pursuits to avert the risk of further trouble, 'We usually talk about my gambling and if I'm leaving myself enough to pay the rent and suchlike', or more indirectly as a signal for assessing potential trouble, 'I always like to know how his hobbies and interests are coming along. It's a sort of indication of his mood'.

Apart from the supervisory objective/perspective link, no other relationships were discovered between the major topics discussed and for example either the officers' or the probationers' characteristics. This was not altogether surprising given the sheer volume and diversity of subjects covered. Apart from the predictable tendency for adults to discuss work, spouses and children, while juveniles usually focused instead on school and parents, no other distinguishable patterns could be found. Neither supervisory officer preferences nor the gender, class or criminality of the probationer were significantly associated. Therefore, regarding the content of conversation, although there was evidence for the presence of a conversational agenda, mediated by the biases identified above, the parameters seem to be too broad for any blanket stereotyping of particular groups of officers and probationers and the likelihood of their discussing particular topics.

The share of conversations

Generally agreed axioms in social work are hard to find but few would disagree with Davies' observation, quoted in the introduction to this section, that the conversational division of labour between the worker and the client should be balanced and not dominated by the worker. Timms and Timms, for example, believe they speak for all social work educators when they state in their consideration of what a social worker should be able to do:

> A social worker must be able to conduct an interview, but in such a way that the participation of the other person is encouraged and maintained... The attempt to discern the worker's part in and responsibility for the interview should not be exaggerated into a takeover bid. (1977 p. 99)

Some axioms are however easier to follow than others and in the probation setting the injunction not to dominate the conversation is especially problematic given the differential power and status of the officer and probationer. As Gahagan has observed with respect to social interaction generally:

> One benefit of superior social status is that one is entitled to initiate interaction with lower status individuals where the latter do not have this right...once into conversation they will have the right to choose the topic, to ask the questions and decide whether answers are adequate, to change the subject, to butt in and to terminate the whole encounter. (1984 p. 62)

Empirically, this process has already been substantiated by Furlong (1976) in her study of teacher-pupil interaction. From her observation of classroom interaction, Furlong found that teachers did almost all the talking, decided whether answers to their questions were adequate, and changed the subject arbitrarily. Could the same apply to officer-probationer dialogues given the analogous formality of the setting and superior role of the former in relation to the latter?

Just as some axioms in social work are easier to follow than others, certain questions concerning probation interaction are harder to answer than others. Ideally an analysis of the share of officer-probationer conversations would have been based on material transcribed from a representative series of unobtrusively tape recorded interviews. Unfortunately, because of the artificiality of officer-probationer interaction prompted by my non-participant observation, this objective method had to be rejected and replaced with a more subjective strategy. This took the form of inviting the officers and probationers to estimate their usual share of conversations in terms of whether the officer or probationer spoke the most, or both talked equally. Although the validity of the results reported here - and indeed elsewhere in this chapter - must remain open to question until they have been confirmed by researchers using a more objective method, the importance of the topic was thought to justify this provisional attempt to clarify the position. While some distortion may be inevitable, the fact that only four of the eighty four pairs gave diametrically opposed answers i.e. where the officers estimated the clients did the most talking but the clients thought the reverse was true, suggests the results are likely to represent a minor rather than major departure from what actually happened. In Table 4.2 therefore, officers' and probationers' estimates of their usual share of conversations is presented as a tentative contribution toward clarifying this important aspect of officer probation interaction.

Table 4.2
Who usually did the most talking

	OFFICERS' ESTIMATES		PROBATIONERS' ESTIMATES	
	N	%	N	%
Officer	21	25.0	23	27.4
Probationer	27	32.1	11	13.1
Equally divided	36	42.9	50	59.5
	84	100.00	84	100.00

Although on a paired basis officers tended to report that probationers dominated the conversations, whereas the particular probationers concerned regarded them as being shared equally, this was a difference of degree rather than magnitude. As the Table clearly shows, in roughly three-quarters of the cases the conversational input conformed to the Timms' prescription. Thus, in spite of the differential power and status of the officer and the probationer, the officer only out-talked the probationer in a quarter of the cases. Consequently those who argue like Harris (1977) for the dissociation of officers from their formal connection with the courts because it is supposed to impede the social work process would seem to be mistaken so far as verbal interaction is concerned.

The fact that the conversational balance was tipped in the wrong direction for approximately one in four of the sample is nevertheless a matter of concern to practitioners - as indeed it was to officers in the present study - and for this reason it was thought useful to investigate this sub-group further. This sub-group was based on all the cases agreed by both the officers and the probationers (21N) and examined to see if any common reasons could be found for their reticence. Were they for example mystified by the subtle nuances of casework (Parkinson 1970), or mesmerised by the catechistic checking of compliance with the conditions of their orders (Walker and Beaumont 1981)? Or were they simply supervised by certain loquacious officers? When each of these possibilities was considered, whatever their plausibility in theory, neither the supervisory officers concerned nor the aims involved proved to be a significant factor in practice. However, when it came to the age and social class of these reticent probationers the distribution was far less random, being significantly associated with juveniles as distinct from adults (x^2 = 8.517, d.f. 1, P < 0.01), coming from working as opposed to middle class backgrounds (x^2 = 4.105, d.f. 1, P < 0.05). So far as the age variable is concerned, the preponderance of juveniles and the fact that all of the few remaining adults were under twenty one corresponds with findings obtained by Giller and Morris in their study of juvenile supervision. According to Giller and Morris, juveniles tended to be reticent because of their 'inability to operate in a counselling setting' (op. cit. p. 155). Many of the supervisors in their sample were reported as stating, for example, that the practice of getting juveniles to delve into and articulate how they felt proved too 'artificial' and 'foreign' for them. Although similar remarks were made by the officers in the present study, this still begs the question why this was so and indeed why some of the juveniles, as Giller and Morris found, did not experience difficulty with operating in the counselling setting. A clue to the reason for this and perhaps the basis for a more comprehensive theorisation of the reticence rests in the class variable and reference to Bernstein's work on restricted and elaborated codes (1971). In Bernstein's view an important reason for the inability of working class children to operate successfully in the educational setting alongside their middle class peers is that socio-linguistically, the former are socialised into a restricted code, whereas the latter learn an elaborated code which is favoured by the school. More specifically, working class children develop a particularistic, context-bound mode of speech, characterised by short, simple, and often repetitive utterances which leave a great deal of the intended meaning implicit i.e. restricted code, while the school as an institution is geared to a universalistic, context-free mode, characterised by long and complex speech patterns where what is said is readily identifiable outside the immediate context of its utterance i.e. elaborated code. Bearing in mind the axiom of balancing if not tipping the conversations in favour of the probationer, it is clear that in the probation, as in the education setting, interaction depends on an elaborated not restricted code. Accordingly, the reasons for the working class juveniles' reticence can be more fully appreciated as stemming from not only their inexperience of counselling, but also the code by which it is conducted. In these terms it is not so much that the particular probationers are doubly handicapped, as the particular officers who have to both generate a conversational agenda and learn the language structure appropriate to its expression. As one officer explained and in doing so alerted me to this process:

> Many of these lads don't say a great deal, you know, you have to dig quite a bit to get the answers that you hope are the right ones. It's almost like learning how they talk, you know, and then teaching them how I talk.

Establishing a common language was not, as the figures suggest, always successful. In some of these cases an inability to operate in the interview setting was exacerbated by an unwillingness either because of the enforced nature of the relationship, or because of a disenchantment with the process noted in the previous chapter with regard to reporting:

> I have to see her but I don't have to talk to her. I just let her yap away.

> It's the same old questions every time, so I give the same old answers. 'Everything okay at home?', 'Yea'. 'Done anything interesting lately?', 'No' (laughs).

From their accounts, in those instances where inability was compounded by unwillingness, the officers and probationers appeared to engage in a series of strategic manoeuvres reminiscent of the information-game variant of Scott's (op. cit.) game theoretic analysis mentioned earlier. Here each party seeks to uncover and conceal certain kinds of knowledge from the other. Sequentially the process commences with the officer being dissatisfied with dominating the conversation. This leads to restating the supervisory aims in a way which attempts to observe what Jamieson (1978) has described as two of the cardinal rules of good interviewing, namely the avoidance of questions likely to elicit monosyllabic responses, and the minimisation of intimidating silences. Both ploys are intended to uncover more information from the probationer. On the other hand, the probationer, in an effort to sabotage the officer's gambit, replies monosyllabically and remains silent thereafter. In addition to the probationers quoted immediately above, consider for example the following complaint from an officer supervising a reticent nineteen year old:

> I know I do most of the talking and I for one certainly raise it from time to time and say 'Look, this isn't good enough, you're on probation, you've got this problem haven't you? We're supposed to be sorting it. We're really both supposed to be feeling pretty confident that this probation order is about seeing that you sort your problem out and don't get into trouble again; or do you see it differently?'. To which he usually replies, 'Well ok I won't'. Silence. End of subject.

Fortunately for both officers and probationers these occasions were confined to a minority. Indeed, in concluding this section, it is perhaps worth emphasising that in the majority of cases the conversational material was varied and more often balanced equally: a complementary finding perhaps to Cohen's (1975) critique of social work critics that 'It's alright for you to talk' in that from a quantitative standpoint, for the majority, the talk seemed to be all right. Could the same be said from a qualitative standpoint with particular reference to the ability of either party to understand each other?

Comprehension

If, as Baldock and Prior argue, 'it is through the doors open to them by speech that social workers enter their clients' lives' (1981 p. 36), then comprehension is the key to the process and incomprehension (to extend the metaphor) the lock which keeps these doors closed. As one probation officer has warned:

> Words are confusing. The same words are seldom interpreted in the same way to two people and the verbally skilled can easily confuse the less articulate. Social workers are often more skilled in this area than their clients and find it easier to out talk them, fill the gaps and fill the client with confusion. (Anderson 1981 p. 56)

In this section an attempt is made to assess whether Baldock and Prior's aspirations seem more appropriate than Anderson's reservations. It has been guided by a concern to address not only whether the probationers understood the officers but also if the officers understood the probationers. Accordingly it acknowledges the view that in all forms of social work practice, including probation, where speech is the principal medium, comprehension is a two- rather than one-way process (Mucchielli 1983, Nelson-Jones 1983). Moreover, instead of restricting the analysis on the one hand to the probationers' understanding of their officers' speech, and on the other, to the officers' understanding of their probationers' speech, an opportunity was presented and taken to additionally verify the impression each party had of their mutual understanding. Thus if the probationers thought they understood their officers it was also feasible and thought useful to ascertain whether the officers agreed, as well as vice versa.

From the evidence supplied earlier regarding the high level of agreement between officers and probationers when describing the general topics of conversation, it may not seem unreasonable to assume a correspondingly high level of mutual understanding in relation to the minutiae of their discussions. However, as Anderson argues, the same words are seldom interpreted in the same way by two people especially in the social work context. Could therefore the apparent consensus be a superficial gloss obscuring a tendency for officers and probationers often to talk at cross purposes to each other? Encouragement of this possibility extends beyond Anderson's reservations to two paradoxes; one applicable to probationers' understanding of officers', the other to officers' understanding of probationers. The first derives from Baldock and Prior's research into social worker-client discourse and the second from Parkinson's critique of probation casework. As will be seen below, both suggest, from quite contrasting perspectives, that the methods supposed to facilitate understanding paradoxically inhibit it. Together therefore they provide important hypotheses to test with regard to the issue of comprehension and indeed the actual as distinct from idealised link between the idea and the practice of probation.

Probationers' understanding of officers: the Baldock and Prior paradox

The first paradox derives from Baldock and Prior's (op. cit.) study of conversations held between a dozen social workers, half of whom were probation officers, and twenty four of their clients. Paradoxically, from the fifteen hours of tape examined, they formed the impression that in almost all of the cases the techniques successfully employed by the workers to enable them to understand their clients were likely to have disabled the clients from understanding the workers! More specifically, Baldock and Prior hypothesise that the workers' commitment to a non-directive and non-judgmental conversational style, exemplified by a 'deceptively casual and relaxed' manner coupled with strategic 'ums and ahs', while facilitating the generation of information deemed important by the workers, probably left the clients confused about the interview's purpose and conclusions because these techniques excluded them from being stated explicitly. It was not only the start and finish of conversations where there was confusion but also their central core:

> Social work interviews do not have a clearly demarcated 'central core'; no equivalent of the doctor's diagnostic stage was discernible, either to us, or, we suspect, the clients. Certainly the workers' objectives were not particularly clear to us until we had listened to the tapes several times and checked our conclusions with them (p. 29).

In the present study the conversations between officers and probationers were not recorded, but unlike Baldock and Prior, it was possible to interview both parties to assess the degree of perceived comprehension/incomprehension as well as elicit examples from them to illustrate this. This methodological difference is important because it may help to explain the radically different findings that were obtained here compared with those documented by Baldock and Prior. In Table 4.3 below, for example, it is clear that there is little evidence to substantiate Baldock and Prior's paradoxical hypothesis. Thus, from a sample of probationers three and a half times larger than that examined by Baldock and Prior there were only two instances where either the officer suspected or the probationer stated that they had never understood what the officer was talking about [3].

Table 4.3
The probationers' understanding of the officers

	OFFICERS' VIEWS		PROBATIONERS' VIEWS	
	N	%	N	%
Yes	73	86.9	71	84.5
No	1	1.2	1	1.2
Mixture	10	11.9	12	14.3
	84	100	84	100

Although there was a greater proportion of cases who <u>sometimes</u> misunderstood the officer, these were still dwarfed by the number believing/stating they understood the officer. Consequently, the obscurity of the workers' objectives during interviews found by Baldock and Prior proved to be the exception rather than the rule for the Berkshire probationers. Indeed when the elaborations of matched officer-probationer pairs were examined, they often illustrated not only the probationers' understanding of the objectives of the interviews but how they related to the officers', if not the probationers', overall perception of the supervisory aims. For example, in the pair quoted immediately below, the probationer perceived her supervision as comprising a blend of support and surveillance whereas the officer thought her offence, which involved theft from patients whilst working as a hospital ancillary, was a one-off occurrence stemming from and therefore requiring support with domestic problems she was experiencing. As the extracts typically illustrate, both agreed that this was a major topic, purpose and conclusion of their conversations.

> We talk mainly about her home, the kinds of things that she and her husband are doing to it and her relationship with him. I think in the interview before last we were talking about her husband's wish to buy another motor bike and her feeling that as a family man he should get a car and take them all out together: but she was just going to leave it to him if that's what he wanted, she wasn't going to oppose him. We've discussed her feelings about it being her home, her family and her money as well as his in the past and I asked her in the light of this whether she thought it was a good idea not to give in, at least before having a series of discussions about it.

> Well I suppose he wants to know if I've got any problems at home, I mean with my husband. I mean straight away you answer 'No' but it's not until you see a person quite frequently and talk at your own leisure and talk about what you feel is going to come next that you realise there are quite a few problems that I'd sort of bottled up. Only sort of niggling or moaning things but they build up. Talking to Mr --- has made me realise I should stand up for myself.

Similarly, in surveillance focused cases the officers' objectives were also usually clear to the probationers, if not always accepted by them. For example, in the following pair, the officer was concerned to curtail a juvenile's principal leisure pursuit of searching for and keeping items apparently discarded in the street because of the risk of being prosecuted for theft by finding:

> We've had some long discussions about the ins and outs of picking things off the street when they weren't his and taking them home instead of handing them to the police. I've told him more than once he musn't do it because he runs a risk of being picked up by the police and searched, and charged with theft by finding.

> Well that theft by finding thing. I understood that but it's still stupid. It's daft innit 'cause anybody would do

> it. If you found a can of coke in the desert you'd drink it wouldn't ya?

Finally, and perhaps most persuasively given the uncertainty assumed to exist when combining support and surveillance i.e. via the vocabulary of care and control, conversations with a mixed aim focus were also clearly understood by the majority of probationers:

> A simple example would be getting work. For one thing it will do your self esteem good, it will do the finances good for another and that it's part of the industriousness clause, you know, the idle hands argument.

> Well I can see the point about getting a job. How I'd be better off than being on the dole. You can't do much on dole money. And how I'd be less likely to get into more trouble if I had something to occupy myself. That sort of thing.

When the characteristics of the probationers who wholly or partly misunderstood the officers were reviewed, no significant pattern could be found to suggest they represented a distinctive sub-group in relation to their own, their officers or the supervisory aims to which they were subject. For example, two of the male officers who thought they sometimes used 'too many complicated words' did not have (by their own or their probationers' estimates) a larger number of confused cases than two of the female offices who felt their language was 'very basic'. Similarly, working class youths may have tended to talk less than their officers but nevertheless appeared to understand them just as well as the other probationers. There was some evidence of the non-directive/non judgmental style backfiring occasionally as the comments of one probationer graphically illustrate:

> He's a right creep, he'll always agree with you. When he talks he sort of creeps around you, 'Yea ... yeeaah ... um ... uumm ...' all the time like that, it's annoying. If he says 'How've you been getting on at school then?' and I say 'I've been getting on alright'. 'Um ... been in any trouble with the teachers then?', 'Well I've been in trouble with a couple of teachers actually'. 'Um ... who are they? ... uumm ... uummm': you know what I mean, all the time, he's a right creep'.

However more frequently the reason for the confusion, and possibly why officers were more often partly than wholly misunderstood, stemmed from the different language experience of the two parties and what Labov (1969) in the educational setting has termed 'vernacular culture'. It was not so much, recalling Bernstein, that these probationers lacked familiarity with the linguistic code or structure of talk favoured by the officers, as the everyday vocabulary or substance of it necessary to understand them. A few of the officers were aware of this to some extent, but from reviewing these instances of partial misunderstanding from the probationers' standpoint, it appeared that just under half of the officers occasionally lapsed into using 'long' or 'posh' words: even so, many other probationers on these officers' caseloads described their language as being 'fairly ordinary' or 'simple to understand'. Overall, therefore, there is little evidence to confirm the Baldock and Prior paradox.

Indeed the findings suggest that the officers not only operate a more flexible conversational style than claimed by Baldock and Prior, but also, when they do tend toward a non-directive/non judgmental manner, the probationers (like the first of the three quoted above) are not judgmental dopes incapable of understanding their implicit purposes either.

As was noted at the outset of this discussion, it seems likely that the radically different conclusions reached here compared with those advanced by Baldock and Prior are related to methodological rather than substantive factors. Two suppositions follow from this, though further research is obviously necessary to establish their validity. First, that Baldock and Prior may be justified in generalising about the prevalence of the non-directive/non judgmental style of social workers' talk with clients: but second, that they are equally unjustified in the inference they make about the latter's ability to comprehend the meaning and purpose of the former's utterances. Instead of these techniques they usefully substantiate constituting a barrier to the clients' understanding, they perhaps more tellingly highlight the limitations experienced by the researchers themselves through relying on one tape recorded interview of 'workers talking only to clients they knew well' (op. cit. p. 36) as a basis for making sense of the workers' objectives. As one commentator who reviewed Baldock and Prior's findings later speculated, and this study appears to have indicated:

> it is possible that the clients were not as confused as we are led to believe, given their long term contact with the workers. (Clifton 1981 p. 39)

Officers' understanding of probationers: the Parkinson paradox

The second paradox originates from a series of articles critical of probation casework written during the seventies by Geoffrey Parkinson (1970, 1977a and 1977b). According to Parkinson the widespread commitment of probation officers in the seventies to the casework method was fundamentally mistaken because, while in theory it appeared to offer the most effective means of understanding clients, in practice it never fulfilled its promise. For Parkinson, not only did the casework method mystify the clients, as Baldock and Prior later argued, but in the process it also prevented the officers themselves from adequately comprehending their probationers' utterances. This was due to what he described as the probation caseworker's inappropriate 'idealisation of clients' problems and attitudes'. As Parkinson explained:

> In so far as they have a theoretical knowledge about life our clients resort to old saws and maxims ... What the worker may not realise is that invariably he is offering the same sort of patterned stereotyped material back to the client only it is middle-class, more 'psychological' and better presented. The client has learnt a fragmented philosophy which hasn't much bearing on his behaviour. The social worker has a psychology more sophisticated but often almost as rigid, which has little to do with the client's real life, or indeed the social worker's real life in many cases. (1970 p.221)

Paradoxically therefore, the method assumed to provide understanding was in Parkinson's view more likely to produce misunderstanding!

Although the eighties have witnessed a proliferation of alternatives to the casework method in probation practice, Walker and Beaumont have argued that these new methods are only 'more of the same' in a different guise. Consequently Parkinson's paradoxical idea of the caseworker's tendency to mistakenly see probationers through an artificial filter of words and concepts remains for them just as acute a decade later:

> Like casework, many of the methods lack relevance to working class life. Family therapy, for example, requires the whole family to meet, focus all their attention on the proceedings and articulate on communication patterns and family functioning. This style of problem solving is no less middle class in orientation than casework and can prove at least equally oppressive ... it seems arrogant to suppose that our working class clients necessarily lack the skills to cope with life, or that probation officers appreciate what skills they do need. Do probation officers know at which pubs men are taken on or how to cope with social interaction on the factory floor? (op. cit. pp. 82-83)

In spite of these and Parkinson's reservations this research found little evidence to corroborate them; the findings summarised below in Table 4.4 being more akin to that anticipated by Baldock and Prior.

Table 4.4
The officers' understanding of the probationers

	OFFICERS' VIEWS		PROBATIONERS' VIEWS	
	N	%	N	%
Yes	75	89.3	69	82.1
No	0	0	3	3.6
Mixture	9	10.7	12	14.3
	84	100	84	100

Thus, when it came to the question of the officers' understanding of the probationers, the vast majority from both groups considered the position to be the same as it had been in reverse. Although three of the probationers thought their officers 'never' understood them, whereas these particular officers were unaware of their being any problem, this was more than offset by the fact that twenty-three times this number of probationers reported being 'always' understood. Like the situation concerning the probationers' understanding of the officers, a more common problem was 'sometimes' misunderstanding or being misunderstood, but here again the numbers were relatively small.

Similarly, the implication from Parkinson, and especially Walker and Beaumont, that support oriented supervisory methods and their filter of words and concepts were more likely to lead to misapprehension than the 'stronger messages' (op. cit. p. 87) and presumably clearer responses of surveillance focused work, could not be upheld. No significant differences were found between the cases grouped according to their officers' supervisory aims and whether they were understood or misunderstood. Differences in perception among some officer probationer pairs may have existed when explaining the overall aims of their supervision (see Chapter 4), but, at the point of assessing the officers' ability to understand them during their routine interaction, the majority of the probationers responding to a support orientation reported being no less or more understood than the majority of probationers responding to a surveillance focus. In this connection, the following two pairs quoted below were typical:

> Well I think he knows that I'm there to try and help him to get re-established again after the breakdown with his girlfriend which led to the offences and basically that's the line I'm taking.

> I've told her problems I've had with my girlfriend and she's answered questions to it. I mean if you don't understand somebody you can't answer their questions really, can you? I mean its not a sort of yes-no question. It's been a fairly long question and answer sort of thing.

> There've been recurring problems with his father-in-law who's apparently a nasty piece of goods. --- doesn't have a history of violence but over the year there've been some dodgy moments and I've had to warn him off a few times.

> I very often speak to her about my family 'cause my father-in-law he's a real pig, you know, no matter what you do, if you got down and licked his boots, you know, he'd still not get on with you. I've never got on with him from the word go and she understands that. She says if he starts something to just ignore him, to keep away from him 'cause it's for my own good, you know, if I hit him I'm in the wrong, I'm the one who'll have to go to court and get done for it. So I've just got to keep away from him, which I have done, I ignore the bloke now. Mind you I still feel like wringing his neck (laughs).

The officers' ability to understand was occasionally underlined by some probationers who pointed to the officers' role as an intermediary, not only understanding the probationer but also utilising this information to enable others to understand the probationer as well. One officer for example, when overseeing and advising on the implementation of family rules, rejected the idea of imposing a curfew and instead defended the views expressed by the juvenile probationer:

> Well he knew what I meant when I told him about staying out late. He knew, you know, boys do play football and stuff like that a lot and he tends to understand children more than me mum because he deals with them.

Not all the children or indeed the adults in the sample shared this probationer's perception, yet when the characteristics of these dissenting cases and the officers involved were examined, both from the officers' and the probationers' assessments, no significant differences between them and those where understanding was reported could be found. It was not the case, for example, that middle-class probation officers were more able to understand their middle- rather than working-class probationers i.e. from the officers' estimates $x^2 = 1.107$, d.f. 1, N.S., and from the probationers' assessment $x^2 = 0.650$, d.f. 1, N.S.[4]. However, the major reason given by the probationers for being misunderstood did confirm the presence of what was regarded as inappropriate filtering, albeit to a much lesser extent than expected and for a greater range of supervisory orientations than implied. In some instances classic casework was faulted:

> I had an argument with me mum and I told her about it and from that moment on she thought there were problems at home. I'd just had a couple of arguments. I mean it's not uncommon. I'd say 'Tuesday I had a row with me mum' - I went out and I didn't tell her where I was going and I didn't come back till about midnight - and you know immediately she jumped to the conclusion, you know, <u>family problems</u>. (L.S.: Which you don't feel is right?) No, I don't.

In others however standard surveillance was a barrier to understanding:

> When I say I don't want to get a job he can't understand that, why I don't want to go out and get a job. My husband's unemployed, I was working and my husband's unemployed and they were stopping me money out of his dole money and to me I just thought, you know, 'I aint working for nothing'. So that's why I won't go and get a job now.

Officers therefore appeared to be equally liable to misunderstanding by filtering their probationers' remarks through either a support or surveillance perspective.

In contrast, from the officers' viewpoint, their major reason for misunderstanding derived not from their own perspective but from the structure or substance of their probationers' utterances. Either their general phrasing or particular wording was unclear to the officer in a manner reminiscent of the difficulties noted by Bernstein and Labov described earlier. The problem for the officers was accordingly less acute and frequently remedied by getting the particular probationer to repeat, rephrase, or expand on what they had originally said:

> Sometimes I have to get her to repeat (a) because of some phrases she uses and (b) sometimes she'll be referring to things that either I've forgotten or I never knew about or she's taken it for granted that I know. But I do understand in the end because I ask her to clarify.

However, this officer's typical response of asking the probationers to clarify what they say may not always be sufficient if we recall the two probationers' comments quoted immediately before it. Consequently, during their routine interaction, officers may need to exercise more caution in reading too much into their probationers' speech. By the same token it is nonetheless important to remember that these instances were rare and caution should also be exercised in reading too much into findings applicable to only a minority.

In conclusion therefore the level of comprehension between officers and probationers, while not complete, was certainly much higher than the two paradoxes might lead an outsider to expect. Whether this was in spite of or because of the criticisms previously made cannot be answered by this research but, whatever the reason, the officers' efforts to achieve mutual understanding clearly appear, for the majority of cases, to have been successful. Mutual understanding is not however synonymous with mutual acceptance, and in the next section this third important component of interaction will be considered.

Conflict

Goffman (1984) has shown in his analysis of studies concerned with social interaction that achieving complete consensus between participants is an optimistic and sociologically naive ideal; even though there is likely to be real agreement about its desirability. In the probation context however, commentators on either side of the support-surveillance continuum suggest that avoiding what Goffman terms 'open contradiction' is not so much an abstract aspiration as the modus operandi underpinning the officer's interaction with the probationer. On the support side, for example, the principle of acceptance, initially associated with psychodynamic casework but subsequently extended to a variety of social work methods (Butrym 1976), formally discourages conflict precipitated by condemning either the attitudes or behaviour of the client/probationer. Biestek, a key exponent of the principle explains:

> Acceptance is a principle of action wherein the caseworker perceives and deals with the client as he really is, including his strengths and weaknesses, his congenial and uncongenial qualities, his positive and negative feelings, his constructive and destructive attitudes and behaviour, maintaining all the while a sense of the client's innate dignity and personal worth.
> Acceptance does not mean approval of deviant attitudes or behaviour. The object of acceptance is not 'the good' but 'the real'. The object of acceptance is pertinent reality.
> (1974 p. 72)

It could be said that officers attempting to apply the principle of acceptance face special problems because of the probationers' already manifest susceptibility to deviant behaviour and conflict with the law. Biestek's second paragraph has probably for this reason been focused upon by commentators from the surveillance side. Here, acceptance is superceded by a concern to ensure conformity to the conditions of the court order. This not only precludes the acceptance or, in casework terms, condonation (Foren and Bailey 1968) of deviation from them, but simultaneously renders them closed to conflict because they are non-negotiable. As Walker and Beaumont have observed, the traditional message of general conformity has, if anything, been

> reinforced by the recent trend towards the insertion of specific additional conditions in probation orders. Instead of encouragement or example, the probation officer can refer to requirements backed by the authority of the court and by sanctions for non-compliance (1981 p. 87).

In view of these supervisory prescriptions and descriptions the results obtained from this research are somewhat surprising; being more in accord with what sociologists, rather than social work theorists, might have led one to expect. Thus when asked whether or not there had ever been any disagreement between them, over a third of the probationers described one or more instances (30N) and nearly twice as many cases with examples were reported by the officers (58N). The difference in perception between the officers and probationers might prompt the suggestion that officers overstated the extent of the conflict. However this detracts from the fact that even on the probationers' estimates much more conflict was recorded than might have been predicted from the application of the principles of acceptance/non-judgmentalism and conformity/non-negotiability. Indeed, when this perceptual disparity was examined on a matched-pair basis with the benefit of supplementary interview and file data, instead of suggesting a fundamental difference of opinion between the parties, it simply connoted a tendency for the probationers to understate the extent of the conflict. Unlike the officers they either discounted instances which in other parts of their interviews they described, or, less frequently, forgot about them even though the particular incidents were clearly recorded in the file [5]. For example, the last probationer quoted in the previous section, when assessing whether the officer understood her reasons for refusing to work, unequivocally implied a disagreement but did not report this later as her officer had done.

Rejection of the idea that officer-probationer interaction is characterised by a static adherence to the principles of acceptance and conformity was encouraged not only by the fact that disagreements were typical rather than exceptional, but also because the issues involved were extremely varied and not limited to a narrow range of non-judgmental e.g. personal life, and non-negotiable e.g. statutory conditions, topics. Disputes were reported for all the topics discussed by the officers and probationers broadly in proportion to their frequency of discussion, with family relationships, work and leisure featuring as both the most popular topics of conversation and disagreement. Moreover, the generality and diversity of disagreements was also highlighted by the varied nature within, as well as between, the different subject areas themselves. Conflicts over family relationships ranged from issues concerning the probationer's ability or willingness to get on with parents or partners, to disputing the custody or access arrangements for their children. Similarly, disagreements about work encompassed whether or not to undertake government schemes, probation work study groups and applying for or giving up jobs: and so on throughout the list of different subject areas.

From an analysis of the various disputes a picture of the routine difficulties involved in translating supervisory aims into practice emerged. Again however, as already indicated in the discussion of non-reporting, neither the quantitative nor the qualitative data could substantiate the view that the common denominator of these difficulties was the care-control dilemma manifested through conflicts arising from predetermined problems entailed in the implementation of support with surveillance objectives. Nor indeed was there any evidence of one type of aim attracting more difficulty than the other. Table 4.5 below, for example, shows in general how no association could be demonstrated between the disagreements reported by the officers and their supervisory aims.

Table 4.5
Officers' supervisory aims and the proportion of disagreements reported

	CASES DISAGREEING		CASES NOT DISAGREEING		TOTAL	
	N	%	N	%	N	%
Support	22	66.7	11	33.3	33	100
Surveillance	10	62.5	6	37.5	16	100
Mixture	26	74.3	9	25.7	35	100

$x^2 = 0.816$, d.f. 2, N.S.

Similarly, the following three extracts illustrate in particular how support, surveillance and mixed aim cases were all equally liable to disagreement. In the first case the officer's unreserved aim to support the probationer's efforts to regain custody of her children resulted in a strong disagreement over what they considered to be the best response to a critical welfare report written by a colleague. The report stated that the probationer/petitioner was 'not yet ready to care for them nor may she be for a considerable time' and recommended the petitioner's sister therefore retain custody:

> One of the things I've found very difficult to get her to look at, you know, to get her to deal with positively, rather than very very negatively, is the fact that she hates the welfare officer. She's quite categorically stated that ... She was going to make an application to the court through her solicitor to change the welfare officer and I advised - I had to say to her that she should think twice about that. (L.S.: Why?) Because if she reads ---'s report very carefully, as I did, she had actually got a lot of material there to help her case, but it needed very careful reading and vetting and picking bits out of. I pointed that out to her and I said 'Look, if you're right and get your officer changed you might have to go right back to the beginning and lose six months or more, is that what you want!?'.

In this case the probationer eventually conceded to the officer but in another the officer's insistence that a juvenile visit the careers office met with obdurate resistance. The probationer explained:

> She tells me to go down to the careers office and I says no. (L.S.: Why?) Because you get in there and you have to wait for an hour before they even see you. Then after the hour they come out and ask you your name again, you know, 'What was your name?' again sort of thing and half an hour later they say someone'll see you in half an hour and you just stand there for ages and ages. They send you off to camera factories and things and I don't want to work in a camera factory. They send you off to all these grotty jobs that you know you wouldn't like anyway. It's just so boring. So I says to her 'I'm not goin' down that place'. (L.S.: And she says what?) She says 'You must, you must go!' and I say 'No!'.

Not all outcomes were as clear-cut as this and sometimes they remained unresolved whatever the supervisory aims. The next dispute, which involved a blend of support and surveillance in relation to the probationer's use of his leisure time, illustrates this:

> We've often disagreed about his drinking. He drinks far too much in my opinion and I've told him so. He considers it to be normal, you know, that it's normal to drink thirteen pints on a Saturday night. It's not just that his last offence happened when he was drunk but I'm also concerned that he could be destroying himself. (L.S.: What's the position now?) He tells me he still drinks but I've checked with people who share the same drinking haunts as he does that in fact he's cut down quite considerably, although it still sounds like he's drinking excessively. I mean cutting down from thirteen pints to eight or nine marks some progress but it's still unsafe.

Overall, roughly a fifth of the disagreements remained unresolved like the example given above (13N) and constituted a periodic source of concern and conflict. However, over three times as many disputes were resolved with outcomes being fairly evenly divided between those preferred by the officers (22N) and those favoured by the probationers (23N). There was little evidence therefore to sustain the critical suggestion that probation interaction is characterised by what Walker and Beaumont have termed, with particular reference to working-class probationers, 'the learning of subservience' (op. cit. p. 83). Nevertheless, some evidence was found to indicate that the way conflicts were managed was class-related, with verbalised disputes tending to arise more often between officers and middle-rather than working-class probationers. Thus, from the officers' estimates, as many as 85% of the former compared with only 61% of the latter expressed disagreement, and the proportional difference was sufficiently large to be statistically significant i.e. $x^2 = 4.937$, d.f. 1, $P < 0.05$. This finding corresponds to that obtained by Crolley and Paley (1983) from interviewing a sample of officers about critical incidents occurring during the course of their civil and criminal work. There were however some important differences found between the strategies reported by these researchers and those adopted by the Berkshire officers and probationers. Rather than reflecting regional differences within the Service, it seems more likely that they signify the exclusion of civil cases from this inquiry and the dissimilar power relations involved in these compared with criminal cases [6].

According to Crolley and Paley three major strategies were employed by 'both sides' and comprised '(1) attempting to browbeat the opponent by various means; (2) introducing a third party; (3) having recourse to law' (ibid. p. 4). In the present study, if reasoned argument failed, officers and probationers appeared to prefer hoodwinking each other instead of the first two strategies mentioned by Crolley and Paley:

> After the new offence he gave up his job and was dead set against getting another one because of his general demoralisation. His prospects were better than most and I was pretty sure he'd be better off all round but he wouldn't budge. So I floated the idea that it wouldn't look good in the report I was writing that he wasn't trying to, you know, pick up the pieces, and that prison had to be on the cards and he took the hint even though I wasn't going to write a negative report anyway.

> He asked me if I wanted to join this club, I forget its name, but I didn't think I would like it. He kept on saying to give it a try but I just didn't want to. It's not that I'm shy or anything like that, I just didn't want to play a load of silly games. (L.S.: What happened?) I made out I wouldn't have the time to go because of my homework from school. It was just an excuse really but it seemed to work (laughs).

From the officers' standpoint, hoodwinking seemed to operate as an informal method of getting their line of argument accepted in a way which did not jeopardise the relationship they were seeking to foster: for the probationers, outwitting rather than browbeating or ganging up via a third party appeared more prudent given the greater power if not status of the officer. When however the disagreement persisted and questioned the continuation of the relationship, like Crolley and Paley's sample, a formal bringing into line by reference or recourse to law eventually resulted. Use of this strategy has already been outlined earlier in connection with non-reporting, but it also arose with three of the adult probationers who expressed the wish to have their orders terminated early because they no longer thought them necessary. In all of these cases the officers considered an early discharge premature and when their reasons were rejected they invited the probationers to take the matter back to court with the full knowledge that they did not have their officer's support. In one case the probationer backed down reluctantly, in another non-reporting gamesmanship ensued, while in a third case the probationer deliberately engineered a court appearance by refusing to see the officer and the order was eventually replaced with a conditional discharge. Hence, not only was recourse to law open to both sides but also from these few cases it appears that the result could go either way or remain unresolved.

The tendency for proportionately more middle- than working-class probationers to verbalise their disagreements did not however signify that the working-class probationer was more submissive than his middle-class counterpart for two important reasons. Firstly because, although under represented relative to middle-class probationers, in absolute terms disagreements were still reported in well over half of the working-class cases. Secondly and more significantly in relation to the manner in which conflicts were managed, just as the working-class probationers' language structure and substance differed from the officers' so too did the way they elected to deal with disagreement. Instead of vocalising dissent many of the working-class probationers seemed to favour simply disregarding the officer:

> If I disagree with 'im 'e might go into a lecture and I don't like that so if 'e says something to me I says yea. If he just kind of goes on and on I just sit there noddin' me 'ead. Most of the time I don't take no notice of 'im.

Or as one officer put it:

> He just votes with his feet. He doesn't actually say 'I don't want to talk about this or do that', he just closes up completely. Voting by inaction or doing what he wants later and not telling me.

When the officers' or the probationers' wishes were frustrated, either because of or in spite of these various verbal and non-verbal strategies, 'the language of character assassination' identified by Crolley and Paley was partially evident from the Berkshire sample. For example, probationers were variously described as 'headstrong', 'manipulative', 'plausible' and 'sick', while a few of the officers themselves were dubbed among other things as busybodies, hypocrites and nosyparkers. These negative epithets were however usually inspired by the recollection rather than first-hand experience of the disagreement and appeared to operate as after-the-event rationalisations which symbolically distanced them from these clashes. For the officers a parallel can be drawn here between this ridiculing of the probationers and the caricaturing of clients by Local Authority social workers to cope with the anxiety of their work (Satyamurti 1981). This difference between neutralising the consequences (as distinct from the causes) of the disagreements seemed important to them because, as a remedial routine, it enabled them both to engage in disputes with probationers and cope with the occasional defeat, rather than deny or suppress the conflict in the first place. Indeed, a number of the officers expressed the view that disagreeing with the probationer had a constructive value, while others implied it through their actions. Consider for example the following exchange:

> P.O.: I don't necessarily think disagreeing with the client is such a bad thing actually. I know you're not saying that but it's - there's a sort of, you know, 'Whatever else you do don't argue with the client!' Sometimes that's the right course of action but it can add realism to the supervision.
>
> L.S.: Can you give me an example?

P.O.: Well we had a bit of a set to about the briefcase, I mean I wasn't going to fork out cash without a bit of a challenge about it, so we had words. I think there was something about his brother had got one, I suspect there was a bit of that in it, 'I'm feeling a bit deprived and I'll see what my P.O. can do about it'.

L.S.: And you had a set to?

P.O.: Yes, I didn't sort of say 'Here you are, here's your money' - 'you don't really need a briefcase, come on they're poofy things!', or something like that, you know, and we had some aggressive banter about it which was quite healthy.

L.S.: And he was able to make his point to you?

P.O.: Yes I went along with it and loaned him the money, but I wouldn't have if he hadn't.

L.S.: Met your challenge?

P.O.: Yes.

Crolley and Paley may therefore be correct in pointing out that character assassinations in the civil work context can instil a false consciousness about the real sociological i.e. class based, as against the imagined psychological i.e. personality based, origins of conflict, but in the context of criminal work the evidence here suggest that they, together with social work theorists generally, have failed to recognise two important points. First, that conflict is commonplace in probation interaction and second, that conflict can often be constructive, adding, in the previously quoted officer's words, 'realism to the supervision'.

For sociologists these two points are not especially new, Simmel having anticipated them in his essay on 'Conflict as Sociation' written at the turn of century (1908). Within social work commentary however, such ideas have tended to be excluded instead of incorporated (Foren and Bialey 1968) with one perceptive exception. Two decades ago Parkinson, in an article once again premised on a paradox, warned officers to beware of co-operation rather than aggression. From the evidence accrued in the present study, although his comprehension paradox may no longer be applicable, his paradoxical remarks on conflict still seem a useful cautionary note with which to conclude this review of conflict and routine probation interaction:

To summarise; the training of the probation officer makes him skilful in dealing with, or perhaps even avoiding aggression. It does little to help him deal with ingratiation. Certainly with the chronic and aggressive offender co-operation should not be understood as progress but rather as a new form of resistance more difficult to handle than active or partially repressed hostility. Unfortunately casework techniques often play into this attitude on the client's part and we must now develop methods that will still hold the dependence of the client on the relationship while introducing an area óf conflict and constructive aggression. For too long many clients have kept 'life' out of probation and for too long probation officers have permitted this. (1966 p. 64)

For those presently practicing the probation idea these observations would seem to have filtered through.

Notes

[1] Perhaps the most serious omission concerns non-verbal communication which, because of the problems encountered when attempting to undertake non-participant observation, had to be omitted from the analysis.
[2] Although in the last chapter it was shown that interviews between officers and probationers often involved others, to avoid duplication of comments made previously this part of the analysis has been confined to the one-to-one sessions.
[3] Interestingly the two cases were not the same although, as with previous comparisons, the difference was one of degree rather than magnitude; the suspected case actually reporting he half understood and the stated case being suspected by the officer of half understanding.
[4] These statistics are based on a 2 x 2 test with the Yates correction because the expected frequency in one cell fell just below 5N. However, even without the adjustment the figures would have failed to reach significance i.e. 2.051 and 1.193 respectively.
[5] From the officers' standpoint this would of course increase their likelihood of remembering the incident.
[6] In criminal cases the state confers much greater power on the officer than in civil cases. Jarvis, for example, notes that in matrimonial supervision orders the officer 'has no sanctions to enforce any form of conduct' including 'the power to enforce attendance at his office' (1980 p. 103).

5 Intervention

The Theme of Intervention

In addition to establishing routine contact and communication, officers have a statutory responsibility and operational brief to intervene directly in the lives of the probationers subject to their supervision. On the statutory side for example, officers are not only entitled but enjoined to visit the probationer's family regularly 'unless there is good reason for not doing so' (P.R. 1965 r. 35 [3]). Similarly, on the operational side, the Probation Rules also include a further basis for intervention by emphasising the importance of encouraging the probationer to:

> make use of any statutory or voluntary agency which might contribute to his welfare and to take advantage of any available social, recreational or educational facilities suited to his age, ability, and temperament... (and) where appropriate endeavour to ensure that such a person is in suitable and regular employment. (ibid. r. 36 [1] and [2])

There are many examples of such intervention, from the establishment of Intermediate Treatment schemes for juveniles, to the placement of adult probationers in hostels. As Davies illustrates, however, they can also involve the more mundane aspects of everyday life:

> phoning the job centre or the gas board, visiting a youth club, placating a neighbour, negotiating a grant, meeting a headmaster, discussing treatment with a psychiatrist, arranging a place in a day centre - all with the hope of

making some kind of impact on the environment for the client's benefit. (1981 p. 121)

However, as Heron has pointed out with regard to social workers generally, practitioners frequently feel ambivalent about intervening in their client's lives, 'since normally it connotes some element of interference' (1982 p. 258). It could be argued that probation officers are especially susceptible to this sort of ambivalence because of the enforced nature of their relationship with probationers. Indeed the same might also be said for the probationers because they also have to balance the benefit against the interference the officers' interventions may involve. Unfortunately, although many commentators have assumed the presence of this ambivalence - often attributing it to the tension of seeking to simultaneously care and control - no comprehensive study of probation intervention has yet been undertaken to confirm it. Instead the studies have tended toward one of two extremes, neither of which satisfactorily clarify the position. On the one hand, some researchers (Sainsbury et al 1982) have treated the whole experience of supervision as being equivalent to probation intervention, with the result that their analysis loses in depth what it gains in breadth. Alternatively, other researchers (Bridges 1976, Lawson 1978) have narrowly focused on particular kinds of intervention such as breaching, these analyses consequently losing in breadth what they gain in depth. In this chapter a different approach to probation intervention has therefore been adopted; recognising its breadth but at the same time acknowledging the need to analyse it in depth.

A useful starting point for analysing the diverse range of interventions involved was found in Heron's (op. cit.) general classification of social work intervention. According to Heron interventions fall into two main groups; namely those which are facilitative, where the emphasis is on 'the effect of the intervention on the client', and those which are authoritative, where the emphasis is on 'what the practitioner is doing'. This distinction, though proposed for all forms of social work intervention, seemed particularly relevant to probation practice because it provided a basis for exploring a wide range of issues concerning both the helping power of the officer i.e. facilitative intervention, and the officer's power to intervene i.e. authoritative intervention.

Accordingly, in the first section below, facilitative intervention is considered in relation to a critical incident analysis of helpful and harmful events that occurred during the course of supervision. In the next two sections attention is given to authoritative intervention with particular reference, first to how strictly the officers operated the supervision and second, leading on from this, theirs' and the probationers' attitude toward and experience of the power to breach for non-compliance.

Critical Incidents

The concept of intervention in social work discourse is not only prone to ambivalence but also ambiguity: often being used synonymously as a generic description of anything or everything undertaken by the worker with or for the client [1]. If we recall Davies' wide ranging catalogue of interventions quoted above, the reasons for this are not hard to appreciate. However, in this section, the concept is explored more specifically through analysing those incidents which occurred during the course of supervision which were thought by the officers and the probationers to have been significant. From a methodological standpoint, distinguishing between significant and insignificant incidents could have been extremely problematic, reviving as it does issues concerning the researcher imputing meanings and making value judgments, but was overcome by utilising the method of 'critical incident analysis' pioneered in the probation context by the Youth Studies Centre staff in Los Angeles. Here, respondents were invited to identify helpful and/or harmful incidents and then answer a series of check-questions concerned with the action taken and assessment made. As Honnard and Sanfilippo explain, these descriptions and judgments 'made by the people most intimately involved...need little more than simple categorisation to obtain useful information' (1961 p. 90), yet minimise researcher bias by maximising the opportunity of recording the respondent's own bias. In the present study officers reported 188N, and probationers 206N separate incidents, consisting of either two or three interventions per case [2]. A database was therefore generated on helpful and harmful incidents which provided for the tabulation, cross-tabulation and analysis of the events, actions and assessments reported from both the officers' and the probationers' perspective.

This complex matrix of information proved useful on three levels. First, for developing a provisional typology of probation intervention with regard to the events, actions and assessments associated with it. Second, for exploring a variety of issues raised by social work commentators concerning the suggested lack of perceptual correspondence between workers and clients - including officers and probationers - whilst on the one hand identifying and on the other evaluating those incidents which they considered to be significant. Third, because the incidents reported subsequently proved to be the major criteria employed by both groups when evaluating the overall progress of their statutory supervision, this data can also be read as an index of the key factors characterising the perceived success or failure of probation practice generically.

The incidents reported

Since the seventies surveys of worker-client perceptions of social work intervention have indicated that whereas workers tend to anticipate that clients will need psychological help with personal problems, most clients expect material aid with the practical difficulties they face (Mayer and Timms 1970, Goldberg and Warburton 1979). Although directly comparable research undertaken in the probation context is scarce [3], the same asymmetry could be inferred from the results of Boswell's study of officers' methods of intervention, and Davies' survey of probationers' perceptions of supervision. Boswell, for example, found that as many as 72% of the officers sampled attempted to achieve their aims by casework methods, while only 20% mentioned practical help (1985 p. 8). Conversely, when describing the implementation of supervisory objectives, only 22% of Davies' probationers identified casework methods such as counselling, whereas over twice as many (49%) mentioned practical assistance (1979 p. 86). From the evidence presented in the previous chapter on conversations between officers and probationers it might seem unlikely that any confirmation of this asymmetry would be found. It will be recalled, for example, how the officers and probationers not only specified and ranked the topics identically, but also how psychological problems concerning relationships and the probationer's personal life were just as, but no more, frequently reported than practical difficulties relating to, inter alia, work and leisure. However, the observations made by Sainsbury and his colleagues, following their longitudinal study of various welfare agencies and their clientele - including probation - raise serious doubts about the correspondence between what officers and probationers discuss during their interviews and what sort of interventions they regard as significant:

> From clients' reports, we found that a narrower range of subjects was discussed as cases progressed, and it seemed probable that many clients ceased to raise issues which, irrespective of their importance, seemed not to attract the workers' interest. (1982 p. 176)

The possibility of social work intervention having more in common with the operation of a lottery than adherence to the principles of equity has important implications. Specifically it brings into sharp focus, as Sainsbury et al point out, the serious problem that 'certain aspects of human need may be ignored' simply because they are not 'close to the social worker's interests'. The asymmetry problem therefore represented an important hypothesis to examine and in Table 5.1 the interventions reported by both groups are listed as a provisional baseline for testing its specific applicability to probation practice.

As can be seen from a close inspection of the Table, there was a great deal more similarity between the officers and probationers as well as variety of interventions recorded than expected. Although, for example, there were some minor differences in their rank order, in proportional terms the type of incidents reported by the officers and probationers were extremely close. Indeed the top three categories were the same for both groups and the similarity of their perception is underlined by the fact that just under half (47%) the incidents described by them were identical. Similarly, a comparison of the topics of conversation and the types of intervention failed to reveal anything approaching the degree of bias inferred by Sainsbury et al. Relationships for example (with or without the inclusion of non-family members) were the most popular interventions, as they had been topics of conversation. Similarly, apart from the original offence which was understandably disregarded by both groups, accommodation remained the least frequently cited category. Moreover, if the Table is reviewed in its entirety, instead of artificially juxtaposing the top and bottom categories, it becomes clear that neither group collectively displayed the sort of skewed distribution toward psychological or practical areas of intervention predicted by the asymmetry hypothesis.

Table 5.1
Incidents reported by officers and probationers in rank order [4]

	OFFICERS				PROBATIONERS		
Rank	Incident	N	%	Rank	Incident	N	%
1	Relationships	38	20.2	1	Relationships	44	21.4
2	Personal Problems	27	14.4	2	Work	25	12.2
3	Work	26	13.8	3	Personal Problems	23	11.2
4	Education	18	9.6	4	Reconviction	22	10.7
4	Leisure	18	9.6	5	Regulation	21	10.2
6	Reconviction	16	8.5	6	Leisure	19	9.2
6	Regulation	16	8.5	6	Finance	19	9.2
8	Finance	15	7.9	8	Education	18	8.7
9	Accommodation	9	4.8	9	Accommodation	11	5.3
10	Miscellaneous	5	2.7	10	Miscellaneous	4	1.9
		188	100			206	100

The possibility of the Table obscuring individual preferences among the officers for certain psychological or practical types of intervention could have gone some way toward salvaging the asymmetry hypothesis by implying a stereotypical split between psychodynamically and environmentally preoccupied officers. However, no such association was found between any one or group of them and the interventions they reported; all describing psychological incidents to do with relationships as well as practical incidents to do with work. Neither was there any evidence that particular types of probationers attracted particular types of intervention. Instead the various characteristics when matched against the various interventions were found to be very evenly spread, as indeed they were in relation to the incidents reported by the probationers themselves. This was most acutely demonstrated by the absence of any bias from either groups' viewpoint toward psychological or practical interventions depending on the probationers' social class. Thus, contrary to the class variant of the asymmetry hypothesis, dating from Mayer and Timms' (op. cit.) study of family welfare clients and since generalised to all recipients of social work intervention, middle-class probationers were no more inclined to the internal world of personal problems than working-class probationers (x^2 = .033, d.f. 1, N.S. for officers and x^2 = .324, d.f. 1, N.S. for probationers); just as working-class probationers were no more inclined to the external world of work than middle-class probationers (x^2 = .474, d.f. 1, N.S. for officers and x^2 = .0003, d.f. 1, N.S. for probationers). Outlining the type of incidents is of course only half of the analysis and any conclusions would be incomplete without a consideration of how they were evaluated.

The incidents evaluated

Defining an incident as significant could be for either positive or negative reasons. Irrespective of the absence of any important differences regarding the types of incident mentioned, recent commentary and research has also implied the likelihood of variation between officers and probationers in how they evaluate them. Specifically, two sort of differences can be inferred: first, that overall the probationers would be more negative than the officers but that second, concentrating on the positive incidents only, the officers would be more modest in their appraisal of them than the probationers. On the first difference Walker and Beaumont, for example, contrast the official with the practice account of probation and argue that while official accounts extol the positives of facilitative and facility oriented work, in effect they are often regarded negatively by the probationer as 'little more than an empty gesture' (op. cit. p. 32). On the second difference, empirical grounds for expecting officers to be more self-critical of their work than probationers originate from Sainsbury et al who, from an analysis of client-worker judgments of the help given and received, found that:

> The greatest discrepancy between the views of clients and workers was in the probation service, where officers were considerably more likely than their clients to judge their work as inadequate. (op. cit. p. 92)

In Table 5.2 below the officers' and probationers' evaluation of the various incidents is expressed along a continuum of 'really helpful' to 'really harmful'. The additional heading of 'neutral' refers to incidents mentioned by either group which, despite attracting a lot of attention, were not considered to be helpful, harmful or a mixture.

Table 5.2
The officers' and probationers' evaluation of incidents

	REALLY HELPFUL		HELPFUL		MIXTURE		HARMFUL		REALLY HARMFUL		NEUTRAL		TOTAL	
	N	%	N	%	N	%	N	%	N	%	N	%	N	%
Officers	51	27.1	95	50.6	18	9.6	16	8.5	4	2.1	4	2.1	188	100
Probationers	73	35.4	67	32.5	24	11.7	18	8.7	8	3.9	16	7.8	206	100

The fact that over three-quarters of the officers' and over two-thirds of the probationers' assessments were on the helpful side, not only indicates that the vast majority of interventions were perceived positively, but also that the positive-negative imbalance between them posed by Walker and Beaumont could not be substantiated. However, there was a sufficiently large difference between the officers' and probationers' distinction between really-helpful and helpful incidents to statistically replicate Sainsbury et al's findings. Officers therefore, if not more negative than the probationers i.e. like the probationers they only placed roughly a tenth of the incidents on the negative side, were certainly more modest (x^2 = 17.163, d.f. 5, P < 0.01). Sainsbury et al were puzzled by this modesty of the officers and speculated that it might have been due to either the probationers naively over-praising the help given, or the officers demonstrating their professional investment in always looking to improve it. The accounts from this research had more in common with the second of their speculations but suggested that excessive self-criticism could be just as inappropriate as the complacent self-congratulation it sought to avoid. In many cases it appeared to lead to a kind of should-because-could-do-more attitude based on either an unrealistic or ambitious programme of intervention. A typical illustration of this is given below. The officer assesses the work undertaken with a probationer whose husband's bouts of 'swanning off' engendered in the neglected wife a passion to separate only exceeded by her passion to remain with him:

> She's needed someone who's not emotionally involved 'er who's not going to say to her 'Leave him' or anything like that but is just going to listen and check over the things she's said and give her the opportunity just to thrash out in her own mind where she goes from here. And somebody who knows her, because she'll say things like 'This time I'm definitely not going to seek him out' when he's hiding in some hotel somewhere: she says 'I'm definitely not going to seek him out, am I?'. Then the next time I see her she says 'I did it didn't I, I went to sort him out and apologied'. So I've acted as a break to get her to stop and think. It's a stormy marriage, he's walked out twice and she's driven a car at him and ordered him out. So I'd say that's been helpful, I wouldn't say really helpful. My work has been very basic, a sort of holding operation, I haven't done any high powered marital counselling, perhaps I should.

The probationer however was much more appreciative and positive:

> I come to her you know um for a shoulder to cry on now and again about my marriage because it's not the sort of thing I'll go talking to anyone else about. Talking it over with her has been really helpful. She knows that even if I come to her completely adamant like I did the last time, when my husband and I are together again and I see her I'll say to her 'Well I did all the things I swore I wouldn't' and she'll say 'Well I knew you would anyway' (laughs). But if I didn't have her to talk to then I'd probably stick to what I said and um end up with a broken marriage which I don' want .

The tendency of offices to undervalue their interventions also applied to practical incidents when, for example, they reported contacting employers for work on the probationers' behalf or, as in the extract below, liaising with the D.H.S.S.:

> I suppose it was helpful when I liaised with the social security to get him his benefit paid after they lost his papers. I backed him up and got him an appointment. It wasn't anything special.

> He really helped me a lot when I had a problem about getting
> my money from the D.H.S.S. He phoned up and made an
> appointment for me to go and see them to try and get it
> sorted out, which I did. I was out of work and needed some
> cash badly.

Not surprisingly, given the correspondence between the incidents reported and the criteria later employed to evaluate the general development in each case, this modesty of the officers was carried through to their assessment of the progress accomplished overall. Thus, whereas only 38% of the cases were regarded as having achieved good progress by the officers, as many as 60% of the probationers responded very positively. Significantly, the 22% difference between the two groups was based on the former being more reserved in their judgment, preferring to designate the progress in these cases as normal rather than good.

If excessive self-criticism could potentially backfire by diminishing the officers' preparedness to undertake similarly 'basic' activities with other probationers, instead preferring more 'high powered' work, they nevertheless need to balance this against overvaluing a few of their interventions. This is highlighted by the second, albeit much smaller, difference between the two groups regarding the proportion of incidents considered to be neither helpful nor harmful. Like Sainsbury's probation sample, officers tended to over-value a small proportion of interventions which the probationers regarded neutrally [5]. One officer, for example, had spent a lot of time 'pushing' a probationer into finding and keeping a job because she felt he was wasting his potential on the dole, much as he had done at school. Unbeknown to the officer however the probationer had left his job, once again because of boredom, and seemed impervious to the officer's original suggestions:

> I didn't find it helpful or harmful, neither really. She
> didn't keep on about it so much, it's just that every time I
> went there she'd say 'Have you got a job yet?' and if I said
> no, she'd say 'Well keep on looking 'cause you know dole
> money isn't much and you've got the potential for a good
> job', stuff like that. She wanted me to see somebody to take
> some tests but I got a job anyway and then I gave it up and
> didn't tell her.

It is, however, important to note that the overall tendency of officers to over-value their work was much less prevalent than the occasions when they devalued it. Likewise, it was more often the case for the probationers to remain neutral about interventions the officers had thought harmful. For example, one officer was critical of his inability to steer a juvenile probationer away from old associates whom he thought had led him into trouble originally and would do so again. The probationer disagreed even though he did reoffend with them, but instead of describing the intervention as harmful remained neutral about it:

> Before I got into trouble again he said I shouldn't see
> these mates who I got into trouble with before because
> they're influencing me and can make me worse. I'd say it was
> as much my fault as it was their's 'cause if I didn't want to

> do nothing I wouldn't. (L.S.: What did your officer do or say to keep you away from your mates?) Well we talked about what I said and my running and doing extra training and joining a club but I wasn't interested.

Because the majority of incidents reported were considered helpful, no significant differences were expected or found among the characteristics of the officers and probationers involved: indeed of the twenty-two cases cited by officers where negative assessments were made, in twenty of them positive incidents were also recorded. Similarly of the thirty-one probationers who mentioned negative or neutral instances, twenty-two also reported positive incidents. Even when the characteristics of the twenty-two and thirty-one cases were compared with the others no statistically significant biases could be found. This applied not only to the probationers' age, gender, class, criminal history and seriousness, but also to the social characteristics of the officers responsible for the particular interventions. Therefore a modified asymmetry hypothesis, whereby helpful or harmful interventions are thought to be associated with specific officer/probationer attributes, was equally untenable. One could not, to take the most plausible possibility, reinstate the class variant of the hypothesis based on the assessments rather than the types of incidents mentioned because, just as there was no correlation between the probationers' social class and the types of incident they reported, neither was there any association when it came to their assessment of them (x^2 = 2.664, d.f. 1, N.S. for officers, x^2 = 0.218, d.f. 1, N.S. for probationers). Furthermore, the view that the psychological-practical distinction would be mirrored by a correspondingly positive-negative or negative-positive assessment - depending on whether the respondent was an officer or a probationer - also had to be rejected. In spite of Kirwin among others claiming that practical interventions are 'not very popular' (1985 p. 41) with officers while the reverse is true for probationers, the majority of each of the different types of intervention reported were assessed positively by both groups. In fact it was quite commonplace to find an officer in the same case describing practical and psychological interventions positively. For example, officers frequently reported aiding the probationer with difficulties over drafting a letter to a prospective employer, getting a grant from D.H.S.S., or obtaining accommodation from the housing authority then, in the next breath, going on to describe if they had not done so beforehand, their help with anxiety, depression or interpersonal conflicts involving family members, friends or neighbours. Interestingly in a few cases, notably those juveniles subject to Intermediate Treatment, the same intervention appeared to fulfil both a practical and a psychological purpose. On the one hand the I.T. provided access to resources not usually available to the juvenile i.e. the <u>treats</u> in I.T. On the other hand it created a context in which to socialise and develop interpersonal skills i.e. the <u>therapy</u> in I.T.:

> His family are very hard up and I think the I.T. has helped get him out of the house and off the streets into doing interesting things he's never had a chance of doing before. He's also learning to mix and improve his communication skills which is no bad thing either.

The most frequent negative source of comment concerned regulatory interventions and revolved around enforcement of the condition to report. Ironically but predictably, officers tended to admonish themselves for not enforcing attendance more rigorously, perceiving their laxity as harmful, while for the probationers it was the perceived severity which caused the harm. Typically, as noted in the chapter on association, the problem increased with the length of the order and in one case matters were brought to a head when the probationer had sight of the Probation Officer's Manual:

> She's got this book about probation stuff, right, and I was looking and I saw this thing, it said um 'Release from probation', you know, and I read it and it said um you know 'Blah blah blah you can be released from probation by (a) your probation officer writing off to the people and advising them to cut it', or (b), right. She told me (a) but she hadn't told me (b). (b) was I could write off to them and say 'Listen, look I've done bugger all wrong, how about it? sort of thing', you know. I wouldn't say that literally but you know what I mean and like in those twelve months she hadn't told me. Now maybe this may seem silly to you right, but like right now I'm doing a one man show and I don't need anyone else; but she says I've got to wait till September. She says to me 'Okay, you write off to them if you want, but I'm not going to back you up'.

Nevertheless it is important to remember that the majority of regulatory interventions were regarded positively i.e. 44% for the officers and 52% for the probationers. In this connection writing a favourable report which told both the probationer's side of the story and recommended a non-custodial disposal was the most popular incident reported by the probationers. Among this group it is perhaps worth noting that one of them was the same probationer quoted immediately above who was later disgruntled about not being able to end the recommended probation alternative to custody early! In two instances officers also mentioned the helpfulness of their social enquiry reports, but more frequently and paradoxically it was the relaxing or reinforcing of the reporting arrangements to fit the perceived needs of the probationer which was thought of as helpful. This suggests that the helpfulness or harmfulness of regulatory activities, like all the other types, depended as much on the circumstances of the case as the intervention per se.

The methods of intervention

The analysis of critical incidents was undertaken not only to specify what the incidents and assessments were but also to clarify the actual methods employed by officers to accomplish them. This was so that a more precise understanding of how they translated their supervisory objectives into practice could be developed. Since Mayer and Timms, commentators may have become sensitive to the distinction between psychological and practical interventions, but this tells us little about exactly how either type of help is accomplished. Does, for example, psychological help, with its emphasis on <u>saying</u> things, involve counselling or directing? Alternatively, do practical interventions, where the accent is on <u>doing</u> things, entail assisting or monitoring? This issue raises three questions which relate to the primary focus of this research:-

1. Given the possibility that psychological and practical types of intervention could be classified in terms of some kind of care-control formulation, how applicable were these concepts to the practice - if not the idea - of probation intervention?

2. How appropriate were support and surveillance as conceptual alternatives?

3. Bearing in mind their presumed conflict in abstract, how compatible were care and control or their alternatives when applied to a variety of discrete and concrete instances?

After describing and evaluating each of the incidents, officers and probationers were invited to apply the concepts of care and control to them. However, as with supervisory aims, there were too many problems to justify their application to supervisory methods. Alternatively, the concepts of support and surveillance consistently served as a much more useful basis of classification. Consider for example a typical exchange where the clarity of support and surveillance can be contrasted with the opacity of care and control:

P.O.: He had a succession of jobs and he kept losing them and he kept coming out with all sorts of reasons like people picking on him and so on. I checked this out with the various employers, after he'd given me permission to contact them, and invariably they said that he was a very difficult person and he only worked when he felt inclined and so on. And I fed that back to him I hope in a helpful way.

L.S.: Would you describe what you said and did as being concerned with caring about his personal difficulty of losing jobs or controlling him from losing jobs so that he didn't misbehave? Or both?

P.O.: It's a bit of both because he wouldn't see losing jobs as a personal difficulty: I did. And it's also controlling because I checked up on him but that was the route to feeding back to him that I cared. I think I was more interested in caring for him. I don't know if it was the right approach but I thought it could be helpful.

Although in support and surveillance terms the officer's account reads as a relatively straightforward illustration of counselling and monitoring, in the vocabulary of care and control there are the problems of conflation and prescription described in Chapter 2. Thus the officer self-consciously and almost apologetically reports his monitoring because actions associated with surveillance are often disvalued, being, to recall another officer quoted in Chapter 2, 'one of the least attractive parts of our job (because it) goes against the grain of self determination'. Officers also had difficulty with applying the concepts of care and control to interventions involving a combination of assisting and directing. In one case, for example, the officer referred a juvenile probationer to a local drama group and insisted the probationer attend even though he had initially refused, preferring to confine his drama activities to school productions:

> Curiously enough, for someone who comes across as being quite shy and reserved, he has quite a lot of dramatic ability; he's done quite well in drama productions at school and I felt I wanted, you know, in some way to cross the bridge between the situation where it sort of happened to him - it didn't need a great deal of initiative on his part to become involved because it was all happening to him in school - to another situation a bit more testing. He'd be with adults for one thing, which I think would test him out, and also could help him mature a great deal. So I went ahead and arranged for him to join a local group despite the fact he wasn't keen at first.

When invited to apply the concepts of care and control to his intervention, the officer thought the concepts were too basic and general:

> I just think it was a useful fairly simple piece of positive directive work that I did with him. I had slight anxieties about his personal growth and lack of fulfillment in his leisure time, and getting him into a drama group was a useful thing to do.

The concepts were equally problematic for the probationers. In 13% of the incidents reported the interventions were unclassifiable in these terms for them, while for the rest the tendency toward conflating or confusing the concepts was often evident. For example, in the losing-jobs intervention quoted earlier the probationer, having described the same incident said:

> It was controlling me so I wouldn't get in any further trouble otherwise it would prove they wasn't caring for me.

As well as indicating the conceptual superiority of support and surveillance over care and control, these quotations also illustrate the compatibility between counselling or assisting on the one hand, and monitoring or directing on the other. This was underlined by both groups when the methods were matched against the assessments for each incident and the majority of mixed-method interventions were found to have been evaluated as helpful i.e. 73% for the officers and 78% for the probationers. There was however an association, again for both groups, between pure surveillance methods of intervention and a harmful assessment. Thus a quarter of the pure surveillance methods reported by the officers and over half of those described by the probationers were assessed negatively. Among both groups these distributions were sufficiently skewed to be statistically significant e.g. $x^2 = 9.934$, d.f. 4, $P < 0.05$ for the officers, and $x^2 = 51.758$, d.f. 4, $P < 0.001$ for the probationers [6]. To some extent this finding complements the results obtained by Sainsbury et al where they found that officers were more likely to be positive about 'the exercise of authority' than the probationers but that neither group regarded it as positively as pure supportive methods [7]. Nevertheless, the fact that 60% and 25% of the pure surveillance interventions were regarded positively by the officers and probationers respectively does suggest that there are occasions when, employed alone, directing and/or monitoring can be helpful; though it seems more so from the officers' than the probationers' perspective.

In the next two sections the attitude of officers and probationers toward pure surveillance methods of intervention will be explored more fully but beforehand the implication of an apparently anomalous result concerning pure supportive methods will be described. In Table 5.3 below the officers' aims matched against the methods of intervention reported by them and the probationers are given.

Table 5.3
Officers' aims and the methods reported by them and the probationers

OFFICERS

Methods

Aims	Support	Surveillance	Mixture
Support	53	4	18
Surveillance	15	5	13
Mixture	45	11	24

Gamma = 0.17, N.S.

PROBATIONERS

Methods

Aims	Support	Surveillance	Mixture
Support	49	7	21
Surveillance	21	5	18
Mixture	59	14	12

Gamma = 0.14, N.S.

As the Table clearly shows, supportive methods were not only as expected the dominant method of intervention for support aim cases, but unexpectedly the dominant method for pure surveillance and mixed aim cases also. After matching the aims and methods on an individual case basis and applying Goodman-Kruskal's gamma test of association, it became clear that there was anything but a correlation [8]. Quite simply, for the officers 53%, and for the probationers 62% of supportive interventions, unexpectedly came from pure surveillance or mixed aim cases! Two possible explanations of this anomaly were immediately considered but subsequently discounted after careful re-examination of the relevant cases and materials. Thus it did not appear that the aims or methods had been incorrectly classified by the researcher nor that the officers concerned had actually contradicted themselves [9]. Instead a third explanation emerged. This was that the interventions reported, rather than rigidly reproducing the original supervisory objectives, reflected the occurrence of and response to events unforseen when the aims were initially formulated. The reader can recall for example the case of the probationer quoted earlier who, having had sight of the Probation Officer's Manual, set in motion a directive response to remain on probation until the officer was prepared to apply for an early discharge. Originally this officer had described the supervision in purely supportive terms. More frequently however the trend was in the opposite direction i.e. from pure surveillance to pure supportive methods of intervention. Two typical cameos illustrate this:

> An eighteen year old first offender prosecuted for theft to the value of £600 was thought to require some form of direction because he 'lacked discipline at home' due to estrangement from his parents. However, during the course of supervision the probationer developed an important attachment to an overseas student. When she returned to her homeland and the probationer expressed a wish to emigrate, the officer supported this by finding out about and supplying a reference to assist in the processing of the official papers.

> A fifty-one year old man with several previous convictions of indecency was originally not regarded by the officer as 'casework material'; requiring instead careful directing and monitoring to avoid further offences. As a result of their regular contact however, a supportive relationship began to develop. This was initially registered and subsequently reinforced by the probationer requesting and receiving help with a D.H.S.S. difficulty he brought to the officer's attention.

Thus, just as officers tended, when explaining the probationers' offences, to take the case to the theories rather than the theory to the cases, when implementing their supervisory aims they remained sufficiently flexible to respond to the changing circumstances of the case instead of adhering rigidly to their original objectives. It would be wrong to conclude that officers' supervisory aims were therefore arbitrary because, as shown in previous chapters, the original aims specified constituted a central if not immutable reference point from which they, the probationers and the researcher made sense of their routine activities. However, this survey of critical incidents does suggest that, in responding to perceived or presented problems, officers are more likely to modify their supervisory style by incorporating supportive methods and achieve positive results from both their own and the probationers' standpoint. In the next section the more problematic position of surveillance methods of intervention is considered.

Strictness

The probation officer's possession of authority is not necessarily an obstacle to casework: it may assist him to exert the firm consistent and benevolent control which some probationers require and many have never experienced.

Before and since this declaration of the Morison Committee (op. cit. p. 23) commentators have been preoccupied with the probation officer's power over the probationer and the tension between on the one hand, official accounts like that of Morison which emphasises the officer's skill in overcoming the probationer's 'fear, suspicion and resentment of authority', and on the other, practice accounts that suggest this fear, suspicion and resentment is just as much a problem for the officer as for the probationer (Parsloe 1979). Certainly, as Parsloe has noted and the present sample confirmed, referring to officers as control agents usually makes them defensive because of their commitment to client self-determination. Indeed this defensiveness could be encouraged by the findings from the previous section where for the officers a quarter and for the probationers over a half of the pure surveillance methods of intervention reported were regarded negatively. However these results are necessarily partial, being based on discrete supervisory incidents, as distinct from the cumulative experience of supervision. Therefore to explore surveillance practices more comprehensively, attention was also focused on the officers' routine exercise of their statutory power to intervene in the probationers' lives.

Instead of aggregating the data from the non-reporting and critical incidents, surveillance practice was addressed in a more rounded rather than roundabout way. After formulating a concept of strictness both groups were asked to firstly estimate how strictly the supervision was conducted, and then secondly evaluate its helpfulness or harmfulness to them. To reduce ambiguity and increase comparability two five point scales were devised which attempted to distinguish between the different types as well as degrees of strictness i.e. things said and things done, from very strict to very easy going [10]. Fortuitously this distinction between saying and doing proved a useful basis for differentiating surveillance through directing and surveillance through monitoring. In Table 5.4 below both groups' estimates and evaluations of how strictly the officer directed the probationers' behaviour are summarised.

A review of the total column down the scale from very strict to very easy-going indicates that, when estimating the level of strictness, officers tended to perceive themselves as being more strict than the probationers found them to be. Just over a fifth of the officers (22.6%) thought they were very strict or strict while under a tenth of the probationers (8.3%) agreed, whereas roughly a quarter of the officers (28.6%) said they were easy-going or very easy-going compared with just under two thirds of the probationers (63.1%). Nevertheless an examination of their evaluations revealed little evidence to corroborate the idea that the officers' directiveness was perceived or experienced as harmful by either group, whatever the degree of strictness. For example, all of the four harmful cases mentioned by the officers were in the moderate to easy-going part of the scale and none of the thirty-one probationers

Table 5.4
The officers' strictness in directing the probationers

	HELPFUL		HARMFUL		MIXTURE		NEUTRAL		TOTAL	
	P.O.	P.	P.O.	P.	P.O.	P.	P.O.	P.	P.O.	P.
Very strict	3	1	0	0	0	0	1	0	4	1
Strict	8	4	0	0	1	0	6	2	15	6
Moderate	34	19	1	0	2	3	4	2	41	24
Easy-going	18	27	1	0	0	1	3	2	22	30
Very easy-going	0	21	2	0	0	0	0	2	2	23
	63	72	4	0	3	4	14	8	84	84

who referred to the officer as being very strict to moderate assessed the strictness as harmful. Among the probationers who estimated their officer had been strict and evaluated this as helpful, a reason commonly given was the underlying message of encouragement to take responsibility for their actions:

> She's said '<u>You</u> must pull yourself together' you know, 'You must do it, nobody else can help you now, only yourself, it's up to you to take the first step'.

Similar comments were also recorded from the officers, central to which was the advantage of letting these probationers know where they stood:

> It's been helpful, because he has faced life, he knows exactly where he stands and that's so important with him.

For the majority of probationers however, it was the moderate to easy-going style of the officers that was thought helpful, and reflected both the probationers' understandable objection to being told what to do and the officers' awareness of this. In this connection a consistent observation running through both groups' accounts was the importance of getting the balance right, matching the level of strictness to the particular justice requirements or welfare needs of the probationer. Being too directive or not directive enough could alienate the probationer and undermine the supervision's usefulness. This point was clearly made by the following pair:

> I've been moderate and I think it's been helpful. I feel that if I'd been absolutely sort of rigid in my approach that it would probably have sent her further away. I felt it necessary to sort of have a bit of give and take.

> I'm the sort of person I don't really like nobody to tell me what to do, you know. If she did tell me what to do and it's to help me out, you know, I would go through with it, you

know, but if she kept on telling me what to do she'd just remind me of my mother and I wouldn't listen.

The way in which instructions were delivered also appeared to be just as important as how strict the officers were with the probationers and to a large extent seemed to reconcile their different estimates but similarly positive evaluations. Harris' rejection of the family metaphor, with its 'activation of the parent child transference' (1980 p. 172), and Mayer and Timms' distinction between introspective and suppressive modes of problem solving (1970 pp. 76-80) are relevant here. In delivering their directions, officers appeared to favour Harris' view that treating all probationers as children, especially juveniles, was profitless:

> I think if you were over strict with --- and if you did sort of go to an adult-child relationship with him he would resent that whereas a more kind of adult-adult relationship has been quite good.

There was more however to the delivery than simply an adult-adult parity. The officers consistently seemed to apply an introspective instead of suppressive style of direction by never leaving an explanation for a particular instruction unstated. The officers therefore appeared to deliberately turn a blind eye to Mayer and Timms' advice that effective problem solving for the working-class client 'relies on deterrence in contrast to one that seeks to uncover underlying causes'. Among the working-class probationers this seemed very profitable:

> Well it helps me 'cause he doesn't just tell me 'You <u>mustn't</u> do this' he sort of tells me why I shouldn't do sort of certain things, which is better than getting shouted at like usually.

A final reason for the generally positive assessment by both groups concerns the context of direction. Among the officers there was a conscious effort to circumscribe their directiveness to matters encompassed within the conditions of the statutory orders. By restricting the field of direction this obviously reduced the grounds for negative assessments. Accordingly, accommodation, employment, reporting and steering clear of persons or places likely to lead to further trouble constituted the boundaries.

In Table 5.5 the officers' monitoring of the probationers' behaviour is summarised. As the total columns show, the differences in estimating the level of strictness were even more pronounced with monitoring than for directing. Over twice as many officers thought they were very strict or strict compared with the probationers i.e. 35%:14%, whereas the reverse was true when the easy-going and very easy-going estimates were combined and contrasted i.e. 29%:70%. However, the proportion of very strict to moderate monitoring perceived or experienced as harmful was again negligible. For example, among the officers these cases were usually assessed positively i.e. just over three-quarters, while for the probationers a positive or neutral response was much more likely than a negative assessment i.e. just under three-quarters.

Table 5.5
The officers' strictness in monitoring the probationers

	HELPFUL		HARMFUL		MIXTURE		NEUTRAL		TOTAL	
	P.O.	P.	P.O.	P.	P.O.	P.	P.O.	P.	P.O.	P.
Very strict	7	2	0	2	0	0	0	2	7	6
Strict	18	3	1	1	1	0	2	2	22	6
Moderate	22	9	3	2	2	2	4	0	31	13
Easy-going	17	21	1	0	1	3	0	8	19	32
Very easy-going	5	23	0	0	0	1	0	3	5	7
	69	58	5	5	4	6	6	15	84	84

From examining both groups' accounts, the reasons for this variation in estimates but nevertheless positive response rate, was found to correspond closely to the balance and delivery factors connected with the positive evaluations of the officers' directiveness. The importance of striking the right balance between too much and too little monitoring, for example, was frequently mentioned by the officers. Usually this pivoted on a joint concern between on the one hand nurturing a relationship and spirit of trust and, on the other, sustaining their role perception as a court officer vested with responsibility for monitoring the probationer's behaviour/problems. Many of the probationers who considered their officers' moderate to easy-going manner helpful, appeared to do so for these reasons:

> I would say he's been fairly moderate actually, in fact no, I would say easy-going. I think it's pitched at the right sort of level for me but I can see that he could fit into any of those categories right up to very strict. I know it's part of his job but he doesn't check up on me that much. I think he takes for granted that everything I tell him is true.

Similarly, the way in which the officers monitored the probationers' behaviour was equally important for two interrelated reasons. First, regarding the style of delivery, a distinction was made between checking-up-on and checking-up-with. Predictably the probationers dislike being checked up on and they condemned this variously as 'prying', 'spying', and 'breaking into your personal life'. Officers anticipated how, as one of them put it, 'going behind their back', could be counter-productive but seemed equally divided about when if ever this was appropriate:

> I check out with, I don't check up on. I would ask but I wouldn't go round to a place and say 'Is so and so here?'. I try and do that with all my clients. I accept their word for things, rightly or wrongly. If they disappear then that's a different matter.

Others however thought this view naive and, although favouring checking-up-with before checking-up-on, felt that covert communication was not only inevitable but desirable:

> Who's kidding who? There has to be covert communication and we often encourage it through the local grapevine; parents, wives and such like. There is, whether you like it or not anyway. People will contact you, the phone rings and you can't say 'Before you say anything I have to check with Jim that it's okay for you to say it'; you can't because you don't know what they've got to say and it could be important. It could be something, you know, the client's conveniently forgotten that has a bearing on what you're doing with him. (L.S.: Like what?) I don't know - truanting from school, giving up work, suspect mates, rows at home, that sort of thing.

The positive attitude towards the officers' monitoring also related to the effects of their style of checking-up-with as well as occasionally checking-up-on. Instead of connoting an exclusive preoccupation with conformity, the officers' checking up was often intended and interpreted as a sign of 'being bothered about' the probationer:

> She's showing an interest, you know, if she never asked me I'd think well, you know, she hasn't got much interest in me.

Consequently, Harris (op. cit.) may be correct to reject the family metaphor as a dubious basis for integrating care and control vis a vis the superior parent directing the inferior child analogy, but there was evidence to suggest that monitoring could be construed as supportive. Note, for example, the comments of the following pair:

> He likes to know that I'm bothered where he's living. He likes to know that I'm concerned how his job is going. He sees me as taking an interest in his life and any problems he's got.
>
> He checks up and I tell him and he can help me at the same time.

The superimposing of supportive reasons on the monitoring undertaken did not however occur in all the cases. Mainly, like the example given, it was found among the officer-probationer pairs where pure support aims were being pursued. In these cases the officers' invocation of supportive reasoning appeared not only to render their monitoring more feasible to operate vis a vis the probationers, but also to resolve their potential dilemma in failing to fulfil their statutorily prescribed obligation to undertake some oversight vis a vis the courts. By contrast, when their supervisory objectives were solely surveillance oriented, reference to supportive reasons was unnecessary because for these cases the officers were only carrying through what they had originally proposed to do and the probationers expected.

Unlike directing, the context of monitoring tended to be much wider than the traditional criteria encapsulated in the conditions of the orders. This reflected the predetermined necessity, whether from a justice or welfare perspective, to assimilate sufficient information to conduct the supervision. Monitoring family dynamics for example, was important as much for gauging the discipline as the dysfunction in the home. Similarly, information concerning a probationer's peer group was not only useful in signalling the risk of further trouble, but also for assessing the progress in reducing social isolation. Although it might be suspected that this broad range of monitoring created a sense of intrusion, the Table clearly shows that this was rarely so. This lack of intrusiveness, from the comments made by both groups, seems largely due to the balance and delivery factors as well as the officers' tendency to <u>personalise</u> their oversight. In turn this appears to have been registered and appreciated by the probationers.

Because both the directing and the monitoring were personalised it was not altogether surprising that previous findings concerning the social characteristics of the officers and probationers engaged in stricter levels of supervision was not repeated. Although Folkard (1966 p. 55) had previously found a statistical association between high control and older officers i.e. those aged forty one plus, who supervised male probationers, neither these nor any of the two groups' other social characteristics proved significant. For example both the younger and the older officers reported strict and easy-going levels of directing and monitoring for different probationers. Furthermore, when the responses were aggregated and those officers with the strictest averages were compared by an under- or over-forty age division, there was little difference in the proportions of those strictly directing i.e. 30%:50%, or strictly monitoring i.e. 60%:50%; the probability levels from the Fisher Exact Test being well outside the 5% level of statistical significance both times i.e. P = 36% and 42% respectively. The same sort of results were found in relation to their gender, training and length of service. This absence of a stereotypically strict officer was underlined by the fact that they not only varied the levels of strictness between different probationers but also between their directing and monitoring with the same probationer in over half of the cases (56%). Regarding the probationers, the inference taken from Folkard's evidence that males are likelier to attract stricter levels of surveillance than females (because they are less submissive or more delinquent) also had to be rejected after examining both the officers' and the probationers' estimates. If anything the estimates tended to invert this expectation of supervisory chauvinism; the strictness being biased toward females in three of the four estimates. However the differences in the relative proportions of males to females subject to strict directing and strict monitoring were so small as to be insignificant [11]. The same negative associations were derived from a review of the strict cases cited by both groups in relation to the probationers' age, class, criminal history and, perhaps most surprising of all, the seriousness of their offences. Therefore it seems that the officers' personalisation of surveillance practice - rather than standardisation - applies as much to the probationers' as their own social characteristics.

Within this wide ranging patten of personalisation there was however some evidence to restore a sense of congruence between the officers' original supervisory aims and their expected methods of intervention questioned earlier by the findings which emerged from the critical incident analysis. Although for example the officers estimated that for the majority of cases their directing and monitoring was moderate, when the extreme distributions of the pure support and pure surveillance aim cases were cross-tabulated a statistically significant bias was found in the direction originally expected i.e. before the results of the critical incident analysis. Thus as shown in Table 5.6, the support cases tended to be concentrated in the easy-going rather than strict cells, while the reverse was true for the surveillance cases.

Table 5.6
Officers' supervisory aims and the strictness of their routine surveillance [12]

AIMS	DIRECTING		MONITORING	
	Strict	Easy-going	Strict	Easy-going
Support	5	10	7	14
Surveillance	7	1	9	2
	P = 1.9%		P = 1.2%	

The officers' tendency to personalise their surveillance practice therefore, instead of contradicting their original supervisory aims, remained more often than not consistent with them. If anything was contradicted it seems to have been the prevalence of fear, suspicion and resentment predicted. But what happened when the directing or monitoring failed to achieve its intended purpose? In the last resort the officer has the power to return the probationer to court for sentencing. To complete this review of surveillance practice both groups' attitude toward and experience of breaching was also therefore considered.

Breaching

Breaching is the most problematic intervention undertaken in probation practice; not only for the breachee returned to court for sentencing but also, it seems, for the breacher instigating this course of action. Local surveys have consistently shown that failure to comply with the requirements of the probation or supervision orders is no guarantee breaching will automatically follow even though it could be justified in court. Officers, it appears, infrequently and inconsistently invoke their power to breach recalcitrant probationers. From his West Yorkshire survey Bridges (1976), for example, found a rate as low as one in every thirty-seven adult probationers (2.7%), while Lawson (1978) in Essex reported one in twenty-seven (3.7%). In both studies, however, considerable variation between the teams of officers contributing to these general rates was noted. There was also evidence that breaching officers tended to delay the sanction over several months or deliberately avoid it altogether 'even though', as Lawson from his practitioner experience observed, 'the probationers behaviour merits such action' (p. 69). Moreover, although the relevant legislation provides for breaching on a variety of counts, both researchers discovered a reluctance among officers to pursue, in Bridges' words, the 'moral conundrums' of failing to be of good behaviour or lead an industrious life. Consequently most breached their probationers for failing to maintain contact i.e. not notifying a change of address or reporting as directed.

Although both researchers found a virtually identical pattern of infrequency and inconsistency, they differed in their explanations of it. For Bridges the pattern was structurally determined and reflected an operational difficulty, reminiscent of the care control dilemma, where breaching the probationer was often regarded as an admission of failure:

> The difficulty in applying sanctions may depend not so much on the personal inadequacy or ambivalence of the practitioners, but upon the operational difficulty of reconciling an approach to the client which may sever a relationship which contradicts the other approaches to the client that officers are expected to make in order to maintain contact. (op. cit. p. 15)

To Lawson however the problem seemed experiential, underscored by the finding that senior probation officers were seven times more likely to breach probationers than main grade officers were:

> In the performance of their middle-management role the seniors have to exercise more initiative and have more experience of taking uncomfortable decisions... It is also reasonable to suppose that promotion to senior, conferring a higher status and greater official recognition is likely to instil more confidence in one's own judgment, and that this will extend into casework practice. (op. cit. p. 49)

Whatever the reason, whether structural or personal, in the wake of the Younger Committee's proposals for 'the exercise of more extensive and intensive supervision and control' (op. cit. para. 289) Bridges' and Lawson's evidence nonetheless presented a disquieting impasse. Put bluntly, it appeared that officers were reluctant even to enforce the standard requirements of traditional probation and supervision orders, let alone 'more extensive and intensive supervision and control'. Six years after Lawson's more recent survey ended and just before the enactment of many of the Younger Committee's recommendations in the Criminal Justice Act 1982, apparently similar and therefore equally disquieting results were obtained in the present study. Thus only three of the eighty four probationers (3.6%) were breached representing a rate as low as one in twenty-eight. Furthermore, in accordance with previous findings, two of the breaches were for failing to maintain contact while the other, which concerned a juvenile, resulted from him not attending school. However, by interviewing a generic instead of breach only sample of officers, the experiences and attitudes documented suggested the need for a radical reformulation not only of the idea of infrequency/inconsistency, but also the inferred tension between policymakers and practitioners.

The primary reformulation prompted by the Berkshire officers concerns the low rate of breaching and the apparent reluctance to enforce the requirements of the orders. If Bridges and Lawson demonstrated that breaching was an inadequate index of probationer recalcitrance, the present study showed that breaching is also inadequate as a measure of the officers' directiveness. One only has to recall the previous section where all the officers reported some direction of the probationer as well as the informal tariff, described in Chapter 3, where progressively directive strategies to non-reporting were noted. Following on from this observation breaching, instead of constituting an exclusive response to recalcitrance, seems more appropriately viewed as a final and logical progression of stratagems. Although breaching was regarded by the officers as a necessary sanction, their accounts indicated that it was equally important to them when used symbolically as a reminder of such power. The need to reformulate breaching practice in this way was stimulated by many exchanges with the officers similar to the one below:

L.S.: Can you tell me what you think and feel about the practice of breaching?

P.O.: We have our own ways of dealing with things we don't approve of or behaving beyond the limits, and we try and deal with it within the relationship. Most people I think have some kind of personal procedure they go through, like they write twice and they send a recorded letter and so on; so the client can get a pretty accurate picture of where he's got to in the process. It looks bad from the outside I suppose because 'er from the point of view of somebody who wants something done about crime, say maybe magistrates or members of the public or editors of local newspapers, 'er it looks soft, but from inside the relationship it feels okay.

L.S.: Does this mean that you don't ever actually breach?

P.O.: No I have, but you need a client who's extremely neglectful of his own interests not to come up with the goods before you get to asking for a summons.

L.S.: Does that make actually breaching an important or irrelevant part of your job as a probation officer?

P.O.: I think it's very important and 'er I can present a good practical argument for that and that is the difference between our controlling young peoples' custody after-care licences and probation orders. I think we have much less power there, say in detention centre licences. We can only write to the Home Office and we know they're unlikely to be recalled. And I think if they're at all shrewd they realise it themselves quite quickly as well and so they, you know, if they've got the nerve they'll just ignore the licence as many do whereas the court is much handier, much more approachable. The clients feel that and we do. I do think it's an important part of the job both for us to keep us doing our job and for them because you think about 'Well

> how's it going to look to the court if I've not seen this
> guy for two and a half months' and 'er you know, I haven't
> been writing him warning letters or anything. I think it
> keeps us going, it provides a discipline to us as well as
> to the clients.

The importance of the symbolic reminder function and the need to reappraise the officers' apparent dereliction of their statutory duty is highlighted by the fact that although only three of the probationers were breached, twenty-one others were formally warned-again mainly for failing to maintain contact - therefore raising the possibility of breach to a rate of one in four. It could, of course, be argued that given the operational and experiential barriers to breaching identified by Bridges and Lawson these were empty rather than real ultimatums. However in every case the officers stated that, had the rebelliousness persisted, breach proceedings would have been implemented and there was little evidence that these barriers were either insurmountable or even applicable. For example, only one of the officers rehearsed the admission of failure viewpoint and ironically this was after not before breaching a probationer in the sample for failing to report as directed. Although this officer had thought breaching appropriate and acted accordingly, he subsequently felt a sense of failure at having reached this stage:

> I think and feel differently. In the very beginning your
> responsibility is to try and get the person to painlessly
> stay within the conditions and if it doesn't work you've got
> to breach. My thinking is that it's rational and logical.
> But with --- it felt very bad. It felt as though I should
> have done better, I should have done more, I should have
> found the key. When I breached her I felt I hadn't actually
> conveyed that there was anything particularly valuable to get
> out of being on probation - I mean I had tried and I felt
> sort of a bit guilty and the kind of self-determining
> relationship bit was gone and all that was left was the
> obligations and the obligations weren't being met and it all
> seemed a cold mechanical logic that led to her being
> breached.

This joint evaluation of both the officer's and the probationer's performance did not however preclude him from, in his words, 'doing the right thing' and for the majority of officers a sense of failure simply did not apply. Indeed rather than denying the spirit of self-determination characterising the relationship, many thought the breach affirmed it:

> I don't see it as an admission of failure. I think if we
> take things that personally we'd crack up within a week.
> Besides, it's the client's self-determination isn't it? I
> think if they have made a choice, fair enough, we can't deny
> them that choice.

If no insurmountable conflict could be found in controlling the caring relationship, there was also little evidence of the tendency to confuse the two concepts as a rationalisation of breaching. Interestingly only one of the officers interpreted this extreme mode of direction as 'a sign of caring', the rest describing the practice in terms associated with the surveillance glossary i.e. 'boundaries', 'the court contract', 'discipline', 'obligations' and 'responsibility'. As one officer explained, however, breaching was amenable to support or surveillance oriented cases:

> In many cases it will enable you to keep the contact necessary to be able to do anything with the client. It will also in other cases make the client aware that they are responsible for their actions and if they don't do what they're supposed to do there will be consequences.

The possibility that breaching might have been avoided because of the alternative barrier of inexperience also had to be rejected. Paradoxically, the only officers to neither breach nor formally warn any of the probationers sampled all had over seven years experience and two were senior probation officers. Moreover, two of the breaching officers were relative newcomers with under three years service and one was a first year officer [13]!

Two pragmatic factors contributing to the avoidance of breach were however mentioned, particularly in relation to the largest group of possible and actual breachees, the non-reporters. First, as Lawson found, the <u>life span</u> of the order appeared to be significant. In those cases approaching the completion of their orders no long-term purpose was seen in breaching:

> I must confess there are some cases that I haven't breached for not turning up when if the orders had longer to run I probably would have and I think that's because I felt there was no long-term purpose in doing so.

The fact that none of the actual breaches occurred during the last quarter of the probation and supervision orders provisionally suggests this is unlikely to be an isolated observation [14]. Second, consideration of the alternatives available compared with the compromise reached could be a potent disincentive to breaching. This was not so much an occupationally ingrained discomfort with prosecuting, as a pragmatic attempt to make the best of a less than satisfactory situation. Officers are not only expected to prosecute non-compliance, but also advise the bench about the likely effects of various disposals:

> There are certain clients that I let manipulate me because when I weigh up in the balance - I'll give you an example. I've a client who's chosen to get a full-time job in an office. She's a mother of four who's ex husband has never paid her any maintenance. Sadly the job doesn't pay as much as it should and I suspect she's slightly disadvantaged but she needs the job because there's an alcoholic history and if she didn't work she'd be at home boozing. She manipulates me like mad. But I can ring her at the office as often as I like and say 'How are you, how are you doing?'. Now I could at some stage say 'I'm going to breach you madam' but what would be the point? What could the bench do with her? She couldn't pay a fine and a conditional discharge would lose the support I can give her. If you haven't got the answer don't breach them.

Pragmatic reasons were also given for ignoring instead of avoiding what is probably the most controversial of all the standard requirements i.e. the good behaviour and industrious life requirement, although ethical considerations were sometimes noted. None of the actual breaches and only four of the thirty-three formal warnings were made on these grounds, in part reflecting, and in part elaborating on the same apprehension with moral conundrums found by Bridges. Two of the officers considered the clause either technically unsound, 'I'm not sure if anybody's proved the correlation between unemployment and crime', or morally suspect, 'It smacks of Protestantism'. Most of the officers agreed that the wording should be rephrased because 'It's very difficult to prove', although thought it worthwhile to retain the clause as it could provide 'a useful lever if you want to get someone into work'. Their preference for clarity is born out by the fact that all formal warnings issued concerning good behaviour and industriousness referred to cases where dissociating from certain persons or finding employment was a stated aim in the original social enquiry report and an integral feature of the subsequent supervision plan.

Notwithstanding these and other subtleties of the officers' breaching practice, the position proved much more consistent and straightforward to those on the receiving end than might have been expected. Of the three probationers actually breached one was positive about the experience and two were negative, yet none expressed or implied any complaint about being treated unjustly:

> I expected it, it was the only thing he could do, he was right to do it.
> (Failing to report: conditional discharge substituted for probation order)

> It feels as though you've got a lead on, it's all nicey nicey but as soon as I put a foot wrong it was back to court, well eventually. I didn't come in and see him for about nine weeks and he sent me some letters. One said if I didn't come in and see him he'd have no alternative but to take me back to court, which he did. Now every time I miss about three weeks I get threatened with the court and I come in.
> (Failing to report: fined £20, probation order continued)

> She took me back to court when I took the morning off school but she was always saying 'I'll take you back to court if you do this'. I thought she was just sort of throwing her weight about. I just did things more slyly after that, more carefully just to get away with it and be one up.
> (Failing to attend school: 12 hours attendance centre, supervision order continued)

Among the formally warned probationers only a fifth (4N) made any negative comments about the warning; twice as many were positive (8N), and slightly more (9N) were indifferent. But again neither the negative nor the indifferent probationers regarded their formal warnings as unjustified and only two of the twenty-four possible or actual breachees said they would abolish the power to breach if they had the opportunity. Similarly, the remaining sixty probationers in all but one instance replied affirmatively when invited to comment on the need for officers to have this power. For the majority it was impossible to imagine supervision without these rules:

> That's what probation's all about isn't it? You've got to keep them. That's what probation is. Those rules are necessary. It's only fair.

This obvious necessity was often perceived in terms of pure support, pure surveillance, or, as one receptive juvenile observed, a mixture of these objectives:

> You have to have those rules 'cause the person could be breaking the law again and there'd be nothing you could do about it 'cause you lost contact with them and you can't make out if he has any problems, you can't help him.

The similarity between the breached/warned and unwarned probationers also surprisingly embraced their respective social characteristics. Contrary to Lawson's findings, no significant differences between the two groups emerged that might suggest certain probationers were especially at risk. The number actually breached is far too small to form any definite conclusions but combined with the number of those formally warned may be substantial enough to underline the impression of the generalised use of breach as part of a graduated system of warnings to all probationers where non-compliance arose. If breaching practice is accepted as part of a graduated system of warnings, rather than an appendage to them, then in managing recalcitrance this small but generic caseload of officers and probationers clearly points to a much less infrequent and inconsistent enforcement of statutory requirements than hitherto inferred from breach-only samples. However, while this evidence may serve to close the credibility gap about probation's soft image with those to whom the officers are accountable, there were signs from those on the receiving end that occasionally the graduated system could inadvertently create another credibility gap potentially just as undermining. Plainly stated, repeated warnings could, like familiarity, breed contempt with some of the probationers. In these cases the exploitation-game (described in Chapter 3) usually degenerated into a form of brinkmanship. This was characterised by the officers being inexorably drawn away from their primary aims toward breaching while the probationer believed it would never happen:

> When I go in she says to me 'If you miss one more you'll be back in court' but it doesn't worry me (pause) it does a bit but I've missed so many and she keeps saying it you get to believe she's just saying it after a while 'cause she says it so many times.

Six of the probationers shared this view following their failure to report or notify the officer of a change of address. Although a very small number, as a proportion they represent nearly a third of all those formally warned which, if applicable to breaching practice generally, must be of concern. Operating the graduated system was not therefore without its problems and one officer's advise to the researcher as a prospective officer 'don't threaten unless you intend to do it' might usefully be shared with his colleagues. Indeed it might prove to be just as important as their preference for emphasising the need to state at the outset the terms of the probation/supervision orders and the consequences of failing to abide by them. In short, it is not only important to know where you stand initially, something which seemed well understood by the probationers, but also to know where you stood when at the brink of being breached.

The argument for inserting the officers' breach activity within a broader perspective can also be applied to their intervention generally. This introduces what, since the labelling critique, has come to be regarded as one of the most controversial and potentially intractable problems besetting the practice of the probation idea. For the probationer the problem concerns the stigma attached to being subject to statutory supervision. For the officer the difficulty springs from the tension between, on the one hand, seeking as a helping agent to minimise any stigma following prosecution, and on the other, acting as a state agent to enforce compliance to the resultant court order thereby maximising the possible stigma. To conclude the review of probation practice the problem of stigma was therefore examined and the results are reported in the next chapter.

Notes

[1] See for example the C.C.E.T.S.W. working groups' discussion of education and training in social work where intervention is employed in this inclusive way to denote the major functions which qualified social workers should be able to perform (1975 pp. 28-29).
[2] No significant differences were found when comparing those officers and probationers reporting two, with those reporting three incidents, in terms of either their social characteristics or the supervisory aims involved: the number of interventions being mentioned by both groups relating more to the individual's own perception and the particular circumstances of the case. The importance of this will become clearer as the results are reported.
[3] Day's study, for example, blurs the psychological-practical distinction by employing a typology based upon counselling and assisting.
[4] The sort of incidents reported were extremely diverse but broadly corresponded to those anticipated in the questionnaire which is reproduced in the Appendix (see 13A1 Q.). For convenience certain clusters of incidents were amalgamated i.e. 'relationships' covers those involving family members, friends and neighbours, 'education' both school and college experiences, and 'reconviction' reoffending as well as keeping away from particular people or places in this connection. 'Regulation' was a fresh category generated to encompass incidents such as court reports written pre- and post- sentence, together with matters relating to the commencement, conduct or termination of supervision. The residual category of 'miscellaneous' refers to atypical and ad hoc events such as receiving a gift from a probationer, negotiating the placement of a probationer in a therapeutic community, and liaising with the Social Services over the custody of a probationer's non-accidentally injured child.

[5] Sainsbury et al report an officer : statutory client 'neutral' ratio of 0% : 3% (op. cit. p. 68).
[6] Neutral assessments, by definition, were excluded from these calculations.
[7] See for example the table of comments (op. cit. pp. 68-69).
[8] This test involves calculating the sum of the positive and negative pairs i.e. contrasting those values inside the boxes with those outside them (Cohen and Holliday 1983 pp. 80-84).
[9] Moreover when the supervisory aims described by the probationers were matched against the incidents they each reported, the result was identical i.e. Gamma = -.33 N.S.
[10] Each point on both scales had a short explanation of what was meant which in turn was cross-checked against the respondent's elaboration to ensure consistency (see the Appendix 36 Q.). Although only one of many ways to interrogate strictness, the scale did seem to represent an improvement on previous attempts to differentiate degrees of strictness by phrases such as 'keeping on the straight and narrow', 'making toe the line', 'keeping a firm hand on', and 'being strict' (Carver op. cit. p. 99).
[11] i.e. for directing 20%:30% from the officers and 8%:10% from the probationers, and for monitoring 34%:35% from the officers and 16%:10% from the probationers.
[12] These probability levels are derived from the Fisher Exact Test because of the small number of cases.
[13] The cases supervised by these experienced and inexperienced officers were vetted to see if either's sampled caseloads were greater breach risks because of their previous history or present accommodation and employment status, but like Lawson no significant differences emerged.
[14] This finding emerged from checking the cases at their completion to see if they had been terminated early due to either a further offence or failure to comply with the requirements of their order.

6 Transformation

The Theme of Transformation

The major contribution of labelling theorists to the sociology of deviance has been the shift in focus from viewing deviant behaviour as objectively given to regarding it as subjectively problematic. Rubington and Weinberg explain the basic differences between these two approaches:

> Whereas the objectively given approach focuses primarily upon the social characteristics of the deviant or the conditions that give rise to deviant acts, the subjectively problematic approach focuses on the definitions and actions both of the deviants themselves and the people who label them deviant, and on the social interaction between the two (1973 p. 4).

Consequently instead of isolating the deviants from those reacting to them, the two groups are situated in a relationship of reciprocal influence as a basis for analysing deviance. Notwithstanding the various criticisms made of labelling theory [1] one of the most enduring propositions relevant to the criminal justice sphere has been that of the transformation effect. Briefly stated this entails a person, once stigmatised with a deviant label, experiencing negative consequences which can serve to perpetuate the deviant career. Although the claim that 'deviant behaviour is behaviour that people so label' (Becker 1963 p. 9) has been rejected as an over-simplified explanation of the existence of deviance, the additional point that deviant behaviour ironically seems to be sustained by the very agencies designed to suppress it remains compelling. Erikson

...le notes that prisons and similar agencies of control, ...hose based in the community i.e. probation:

...ide aid and shelter to large numbers of deviant persons, ...metimes enhancing their survival chances in the world as a whole. But beyond this, such institutions gather marginal people into tightly segregated groups, give them an opportunity to teach one another the skills and attitudes of a deviant career, and often provoke them into employing these skills by reinforcing their sense of alienation from the rest of society. (1964 p. 15)

However, in the British criminal justice system the empirical evidence substantiating this 'secondary deviance' (Lemert 1967) is extremely sparse. Indeed for adult probation and juvenile supervision it is non-existent. As Parsloe has observed, the only certainty appears to be how the labelling critique has undermined the officers' morale by encouraging them to 'seek refuge in the so-called strategies of non-intervention' (1979 p. 27). This irony of officers seeming to accept uncritically such a fundamental critique of their practice before it has been demonstrated empirically can partly be explained by the persuasive logic of labelling theory, and partly because of the difficulty in rigorously testing for its existence. It is all very well to suggest, for example, that given the officers' aims to support and survey probationers the negative consequences would be in the former, the creation of dependence, and in the latter, the breakdown of trust, but what are the appropriate criteria necessary for their measurement? Furthermore would they be sufficient as a basis for documenting the various strands of secondary deviance proposed by labelling theorists? Although these questions merit another research project, a way forward was found from Walker's (1980) comprehensive outline of what amount to seven propositions relevant to the process of secondary deviance and the issue of stigma. In summary the propositions are as follows:-

1. <u>Suspicion</u> - offenders may become more likely to be suspected of subsequent offences.

2. <u>Employment</u> - they may find it harder to get or keep a legitimate job.

3. <u>Ostracism</u> - they may lose friends or even their family's support and seek the company of law breakers.

4. <u>Damaged self-image</u> - they may internalise the label, assume it to be their nature and act accordingly.

5. <u>Anti-label reaction</u> - alternatively they may reject the label as unfair and so behave more, instead of less, correctly.

6. <u>Anti-labeller reaction</u> - they may react against the labeller rather than the label and devote themselves to exposing the vices of the establishment.

7. <u>Martyrdom</u> - in some instances the offender and others may consider the sentence a great moral wrong and campaign against it (ibid. pp. 143-144).

Even though Walker took the view that the empirical work undertaken hitherto has been 'scrappy and equivocal' his typology nevertheless provided a useful analytic framework to initiate a more systematic investigation based on data obtained in the present study. Initially, both groups were invited to estimate the proportion of persons the probationers knew who were aware of them being subject to supervision. After this, they were asked to evaluate how, and especially in what way, this was helpful or harmful. Having grouped their various responses according to the seven propositions, it then became possible not only to review the general issue of stigma but also to assess the particular problem addressed throughout this inquiry i.e. the care/helping-agent versus control/state-agent dilemma [2].

General Findings

Although the results described here cannot be considered conclusive, they nevertheless raise doubts about the conclusiveness of the stigmatic effects of statutory supervision. This sceptical view derives from the fact that even though over three-quarters of both groups estimated 'some', 'most', or 'all' of those with whom the probationer had contact knew they were under supervision, the proportion of purely negative experiences registered was much smaller than expected. Indeed, as Table 6.1 below shows, this was not the only unexpected result.

Table 6.1
The consequences of people knowing the probationer was under supervision

TYPE OF EXPERIENCE	OFFICERS' REPORTS		PROBATIONERS' REPORTS	
	N	%	N	%
Negative	38	45.2	45	53.6
Positive	6	7.2	7	8.3
Mixed	9	10.7	5	6.0
Neutral	31	36.9	27	32.1
	84	100	84	100

Thus, many of the experiences reported were regarded neutrally and some were even considered to be either partly or wholly positive. Equally surprising, and all the more striking because of the officers' and probationers' broad similarity in perception, was the absence of any association from both groups' perspective between those cases where purely negative experiences were reported and either their social characteristics or the supervisory aims to which they were subject. Regarding the probationers' characteristics, this was most acutely demonstrated by an examination of the probationers' criminal history. Whereas the logic of labelling would, if nothing else, lead one to expect significant differences between first offenders and recidivists [3] - in accordance with the idea that repeated exposure to the criminalisation process results in greater stigmatisation - neither the officers' nor the probationers' comments could confirm this. Ironically, the distribution of replies was in the opposite direction to that expected, but the difference was well below justifying the counter-claim that first offenders were more vulnerable than hardened recidivists i.e. 40%:43% for the officers, and 50%:54% for the probationers. Similarly, the expectation that the more serious the offence the greater the likelihood of stigma was also not upheld statistically by either group when the negative or other experiences of the most and least serious offenders were compared ($x^2 = 0.432$, d.f. 1, N.S. for officers, and $x^2 = 0.692$, d.f. 1, N.S. for probationers). The tendency for the probationers' characteristics to be fairly evenly distributed in relation to the purely negative and indeed other experiences was also found when the officers' supervisory aims were compared with the types of experiences reported by themselves and the probationers directly. For example, in line with the general distribution of negative experiences, support, surveillance and mixed aim cases for the officers each amounted to just under half of their respective totals while for the probationers the corresponding proportion, again like the position overall, was just over a half. However as will be seen later, supervisory aims still appeared to be important in influencing the type, as distinct from the evaluation, of effects experienced.

Before outlining the nature of these experiences two caveats are necessary concerning Walker's typology and the use made of it here. First, because it was formulated as a conceptual tool for organising a diversity of ideas applied to the criminalisation process generally, it inevitably lacked the empirical detail derived from a focus on one of the various agencies involved. Therefore, in the light of the comments made by both the officers and probationers, instead of squeezing their responses into the existing typology it was thought more appropriate to extend and refine it. Second, because Walker's typology was intended as a framework for analysing the consequences of conviction as distinct from the effects of supervision, it could be argued that its transposition to the probation context is illegitimate. However, because the questions were geared toward eliciting evidence directly related to being under supervision, the subsequent fit between the modified typology and the emergent data appeared to vindicate rather than deny the validity of the transposition. Nevertheless among the purely negative cases recorded many did say that it was the knowledge of a conviction not the statutory supervision which was harmful i.e. 27% of them from the officers' standpoint and 20% from the probationers'. This therefore implies that, notwithstanding the fact that the latter is impossible without the former, the negative effects of the officers' supervisory work are even less marked than already described.

Suspicion

By the completion of their orders twenty of the probationers had been reconvicted and during the fieldwork interviews a further ten admitted reoffending, even though they had escaped detection. At least a third of the probationers sampled [4] could therefore have been justifiably suspected of committing further offences; yet only three to the officers' knowledge and six of the probationers themselves reported contact from the police immediately after the commission of these offences. The number of unjustly suspected cases was similarly small, the officers citing six cases which brought their total of those suspected up to nine while four of the probationers complained of unjust suspicion bringing their total up to ten. Consequently, in spite of its notoriety, the stigma of suspicion did not appear to constitute the problem predicted by labelling theory. Indeed it was only ranked by both groups as being fourth in order of troublesomeness, affecting as little as a sixth of the sample based on the fourteen separate cases where it was reported by the officer and/or the probationer. Moreover, the asserted problem of police suspicion was also dissipated by two other discoveries. Firstly, in five of the instances mentioned i.e. based on three separate cases, the suspicious third party was not the police. Secondly and unexpectedly, on ten other occasions i.e. based on nine separate cases, positive instead of negative experiences were described. It seems that suspicion could and did extend to other statutory agencies and members of the probationer's family. As with the police, however, the apparent liability of being under supervision could be transformed into an asset. In one case, for example, an officer was able to intervene on behalf of a homeless probationer and assist her to obtain council accommodation. This transformation of an apparently hopeless application was accomplished by the officer through reassuring the authorities that their suspicion of her returning to a nomadic existence was groundless because of the support available from the officer. Similarly, just under half of the officers stated that in preventive terms, especially among those cases where surveillance aims were prominent, suspicion by the police had a deterrent value that could be utilised positively during supervision:

> He's often suspected and it reminds him that he does have a label: but as I'm trying to get through to him now, just because he's suspected doesn't mean he's guilty, and if he can prove his innocence by not offending that's all he has to do to lose the label. It's up to him and I think his dealings with the police indirectly help to reinforce that.

Given that four of the six reoffending probationers suspected by the police reoffended twice, including the case cited by the officer above, the deterrent value of police contact is questionable. Nevertheless the typical complaint voiced by this particular probationer of feeling 'a marked man', in the light of the repeated offending, seems more akin to sour grapes than an indication of harassment.

This is not however to deny the existence of unjust suspicion and occasions where, irrespective of the officer's efforts, negative experiences were encountered. The complaint, for example, that every time something went missing from home they were automatically accused by suspicious parents because of their previous theft offences, was reported by two of the juveniles, both of whom protested their innocence enough to satisfy their officers. Unfortunately for both of them, the officers' attempts to act as buffers and foster a spirit of trust only served to fuel the suspicion further. As one of the aggrieved probationers said, 'They reckon that if I was honest I wouldn't need a probation officer'. These and other instances where home visits were made by the police, heavy-handedly looking for evidence to incriminate the innocent probationer in front of other family members, while acute for the individuals concerned, were still relatively infrequent. As will be seen below they were also much less of a problem than found with getting or keeping a legitimate job.

Employment

When the original offences were committed forty-one of the probationers were eligible for employment. Twenty-one were employed and twenty unemployed. By the time fieldwork interviews were held various job swaps, gains and losses had occurred but if anything the overall position looked better than before with twenty-six employed and fifteen unemployed. However, as Ericson's (1977) study of offenders discharged from detention centre has shown, simply comparing the proportion employed and unemployed can obscure the extra effort required and difficulties encountered in gaining employment for the ex-offender. Here also the figures are misleading because, in spite of the overwhelmingly favourable response from both officers and probationers concerning employment focused interventions described earlier, only two separate cases reported positive experiences attributable to employers being told they were under supervision. By contrast in fifteen other cases negative encounters were recorded. Employers therefore constituted a problem for over a third of those eligible for work. Ericson's finding that the ex-inmates had more problems with keeping than getting 'bottom rung' jobs did not apply to the probationers whose main problem, following their higher aspirations, was in obtaining a job they and their officers felt they were suited to. Like the ex-inmates however, and unlike the other aspects of stigma reviewed, having a record rather than being under supervision usually appeared to be the deciding factor. Because the entry or return to employment tended to be at least one rung up from the bottom and part of a broader process of rehabilitation, the probationers faced a dual problem. First, failure to disclose they had a criminal record conflicted with the 'good behaviour' requirement that is coupled with the 'industrious' clause of the orders. Second, even if, as many admitted, they did conceal their record - occasionally with their officers' connivance- there was still the further problem of presenting their previous unemployment or employment in an acceptable light:

> No one ever asks you if you're on probation, they just say- you know on the form is 'Have you been a criminal?' I always miss that part out. --- (P.O.) says I should and bring it up at the interview but I never do now. I know it's wrong but yunno it can backfire on you, it's happened to me loads of times (laughs) it's even happened when I didn't tell 'em. I was gonna be a postman but you see 'cause I lied so much, 'cause I had to cover up all these gaps in my life where I'd been away. So I give 'im all these fairy tale jobs yunno and he took one look and said 'You've had so many jobs you're unreliable so 'op it' sort of thing.

Against this background the references provided by the officers which helped secure employment for two of the probationers tended to be overshadowed. However it would be equally wrong to lose sight of the fact that not all employers were prejudiced against offenders, particularly those who already employed them. Indeed in five cases where the employers knew about the offences before the court hearing, the offenders not only kept their jobs but two of them also received testimonials from their employers which helped them obtain supervision!

The situation does still remain relatively gloomy for many probationers, having extra hurdles placed in their way compared with unconvicted persons. Furthermore the position is little better for those at school. Out of seven separate cases only one positive experience was reported and this came from an officer without verification from the juvenile concerned. In contrast the rest complained and their officers acknowledged how they were often 'picked on' by certain teachers who were quick to engineer an excuse to suspend or expel them:

> Some of the teachers resent like hell the ---'s of this world being there. One gives him a lot of stick and makes an example of him in front of the class. 'Our young delinquent over there'. Quite unnecessary. It's a constant battle to keep on top of it and frankly I don't think I'm winning.

Taken together the problems experienced attending school or applying for jobs was ranked in order of troublesomeness as being second by the officers and third by the probationers. Even more troublesome for the latter though was the problem of ostracism.

Ostracism

The negative experiences associated with suspicion and employment contributed to and overlapped with the problem of social distancing between probationers and members of the community. However this process of ostracism proved more pervasive than anticipated by Walker and extended beyond the family and friendship networks he suggests. There were, for example, instances cited by the sample of family members rejecting the probationers as the 'black sheep' and friends disowning them as 'troublemakers', but various officials and neighbours were also implicated. Interestingly the officers' and probationers' perception of both the numbers involved and sources of ostracism differed markedly. Although in total there were twenty-six separate cases where it was reported, nineteen of these were volunteered by the probationers compared with only ten from the officers. Moreover as few as three of the cases mentioned by the officers were also reported by the probationers themselves. From the officers' perspective nearly two-thirds of the ostracism derived from various officials such as a bank manager arbitrarily refusing to make a loan, a G.P. dubiously withholding services, and housing officers unreasonably rejecting applications to move out of sub-standard accommodation. From the probationers' standpoint however, the major problem was with neighbours and accounted for just under half of their complaints. Accordingly when each of the different manifestations of stigma-related problems were compared, the officers appeared to be least sensitive to the problem of ostracism, particularly so far as neighbours were concerned. This was brought into sharp focus in one case where the officer enlisted a volunteer to provide some practical support to a probationer and suggested visiting her at home. On finding the probation out, instead of leaving a calling card, the volunteer visited a local pub and, failing to locate her their either, seemed to settle for publicising the reason for the visit. The probationer explains the consequences of this:

> The landlord of the pub loves this sort of thing happening. It was very very embarrassing being talked about by everyone in the pub and getting those knowing looks about me being on probation. I wrote to --- (P.O.) and complained and she wrote back saying how sorry she was about it, but the damage had been done.

This was an extreme case but nonetheless illustrates a common thread running through all the instances of ostracism recounted. With or without their officers' aid, and irrespective of how hard the probationers attempted to disclaim their discredited identity, families, friends and especially neighbours and officials were quick to stereotype them with the degraded status researchers have shown begins at the court appearance (Garfinkel 1956, Carlen 1976). It is important however to remember this problem did not affect over two thirds of the probationers, and that there was little evidence to substantiate the idea that ostracism impelled the probationers into the exclusive company of delinquent peers and a delinquent way of life [5]. Ironically, this idea was overturned by the discovery of a trend in the opposite direction. Thus seven of the probationers, including two who reported negative experiences with neighbours, described incidents where their friends actively discouraged them from engaging in further trouble!

Damaged Self-image

Damage to their self-image was equally troublesome for the probationers as ostracism, and by far the most extensive problem perceived by the officers. Overall, thirty-eight separate cases were reported i.e. twenty-four from the officers and nineteen from the probationers. Although there were only four cases where officers and probationers jointly identified the problem, the large number cited by the officer-group clearly indicated their awareness of this problem. Again however the problem proved to be more complex than suggested by Walker's typology, especially in relation to the proposition advanced by Lemert that:

> Something happens 'inside the skin' of the deviant person...as a consequence of having been made the subject of 'treatment' or 'rehabilitation'. The individual's perception of values, means and estimate of their costs undergoes revisions in such ways that... engender responses contrary to those sought by others (1967 p. 17).

For both groups this paradoxical equation of rehabilitation equalling secondary deviation was too general. In the officers' view, damage to the probationer's self-image, instead of being uniform, entailed problems relating to _either_ fame _or_ shame. This not only involved quite different types of experience but had significant ramifications for future conduct. Compare for example the comments from one of the officers about two cases where the backgrounds and offences were virtually identical but the types of experience differed dramatically:

> It's no shame to her. More like kudos. She's proud of being on supervision. It's the borstal boy syndrome, you know, 'I've been to borstal, I'm tougher than you'. It's the same with her on a different scale.
>
> She's got quite a proper sense of shame, I don't think it's something she's strictly proud of but of course that may be helpful to her as it happens. It may act as a sort of sanction and keep her out of trouble.

Whereas in the first case the officer was worried that the perceived fame of being on supervision would precipitate further offending, in the second, the shame was interpreted as a helpful basis for avoiding it. By the completion of their orders the first case had reoffended while the second had not and this exemplifies what was found to be a general trend. In Table 6.2 the thirty-eight fame and shame cases are divided according to whether they reoffended.

Table 6.2
Type of damaged self-image and reoffending *

	BROKE LAW	KEPT LAW
Fame	10	7
Shame	5	16
	15	23

$x^2 = 4.856$, d.f. 1, $P < 0.05$

* This includes self reported as well as officially recorded offending.

This not entirely surprising pattern may come as a mixture of concern and relief to practitioners: concern that in nearly two out of three cases where fame was present further offending resulted, but relief that for three out of four experiencing shame it did not. This relief can be additionally reinforced by the positive overall finding that neither effect was noted in over half of the sample.

Anti-Label/Labeller Reactions and Martyrdom

In total there was only a handful of cases falling under these three heads and possibly reflects the generally low incidence of these particular problems. For example only one instance of martydom was noted. This involved a probationer feeling indignant about being convicted of criminal damage. He had smashed the door and window of his ex-girlfriend's house to try to speak with her about the 'bad influence' he believed local American servicemen, whom she was seeing, were having on her and their baby daughter. This is hardly the basis for a sociology of probationer martydom. Similarly only one example of an anti-labeller reaction was identified and this was directed by a juvenile probationer toward his school teachers not his officer. Indeed the probationer formed an alliance with the officer to challenge their view that his punk hairstyle was 'racialist' and a justification for banning him from school.

There were however three cases of an anti-label reaction and, although a minority, they did show how officers in cases involving extremely stigmatised offences i.e. child abuse and gross indecency, either intentionally or inadvertently reinforce the probationers' zealousness to behave almost over-correctly. One of these probationers, for example, went to great pains to return some cash given to him by members of a sex offenders group he attended even though they had originally offered him the money as a gift. The officer, instead of dissuading the probationer, lavished praise on his ability and willingness to repay the sum. He explained that this helped to reinforce the probationers' commitment to repay, metaphorically as well as literally, what he perceived as his debt to the community. This and other examples noted were nevertheless too few to draw any firm conclusions and possibly require more focused study.

In concluding this review of the theme of transformation, and indeed the general practice of the probation idea, it is perhaps timely to consider the comments of George Herbert Mead from whom the major labelling theorists took their lead. For Mead, contemporary methods of dealing with the offender were doomed by a double bind like the care-control dilemma with which this inquiry began:

> The two attitudes, that of control of crime by the hostile procedure of the law and that of control through comprehension of social and psychological conditions, cannot be combined. To understand is to forgive and the social procedure seems to deny the very responsibility which the law affirms and on the other hand the pursuit by criminal justice inevitably awakens the hostile attitude in the offender and renders the attitude of mutual comprehension practically impossible (1918 p. 592).

From the evidence presented in this and preceding chapters Mead's double bind, like the one applied to the probation context, appears to have been fundamentally misconceived. To understand is not to condone and therefore cause a conflict between comprehending and censuring. Rather it is to signal the hallmark of what Foucault has described as the 'age of examinatory justice' (1977 p. 305). Nowadays to know is a necessary condition for criminal justice and within which probation support and surveillance presently operate. As one of the officers objecting to the pessimism of labelling theory remarked rhetorically, 'Surely it depends on what is done during supervision?' From the fieldwork undertaken here this would certainly seem to be the case. Furthermore, in so far as what is done derives from the support-surveillance continuum of aims, neither the methods nor the effects of doing supervision, including the issue of stigma, seem to be as problematic as presumed hitherto.

Notes

[1] See Plummer (1979) for a comprehensive and critical review.
[2] Although the main source of data for this item derived from the question concerning how many persons known to the probationers knew they were subject to supervision, useful information was also generated from other questions and was therefore incorporated in the analysis. This was particularly so for the question about the importance of supervision in the probationer's life.
[3] A recidivist was defined here as an offender with three or more previous convictions.
[4] i.e. more may have reoffended and escaped detection either before or after the interviews were conducted.
[5] When the ostracised and the non-ostracised cases were assessed to see if they had or had not reoffended - including officially and unofficially recorded crimes - the result was not statistically significant i.e. $x^2 = 0.119$, d.f. 1, N.S.

7 Conclusion

Towards a New Perspective for Probation Practice

This research commenced by defining a succession of questions concerned to elucidate probation practice but has concluded by questioning many definitions of its aims, methods and effects provided hitherto. At the root of the analysis prompting this conclusion and from which a series of related themes came to be explored was the critical interrogation of the care-control dilemma. In spite of the centrality and importance accorded to the concepts of care and control within probation discourse, the preceding chapters have shown that, as a basis for either explaining the idea or describing the practice of doing supervision, they invariably confuse instead of clarify our understanding.

In Chapter 2, where the sample's assessment and elaboration of what the concepts meant to them was reported, six problems were identified; namely inaccuracy, inadequacy, variation, conflation, confusion and prescription. Eliciting the officers' and probationers' understanding of the idea of probation practice was however instrumental in formulating the alternative and more satisfactory concepts of support and surveillance. The superiority of these alternative concepts was initially indicated by their ability to avoid the six problems associated with care and control. For example, problems concerning the misleading nature of the care and control concepts, as well as their generality and indistinguishability from each other i.e. inaccuracy, inadequacy and conflation, were avoided through identifying four specific and recurring objectives in the officers' and probationers' accounts which could be related to the overarching supervisory aims of support i.e. counselling and assisting, and surveillance i.e. directing and monitoring. Similarly, problems arising from the diffuse and inverted usage of care and control i.e. variation and confusion, were overcome through the development of an eight- rather than four-fold typology of supervisory aims which acknowledged not only the need for conceptual precision but also the influence of the welfare and justice orientations toward the idea of probation practice. Finally, the superiority of support and surveillance in depicting actual supervisory aims, as opposed to denoting value judgments about what they ought to be i.e. the problem of prescription, was perhaps best illustrated by their helpfulness in identifying and analysing a new dilemma for the idea of probation practice hitherto eclipsed by care-control debaters. This dilemma, discussed at the close of Chapter 2, concerned a number of cases where discrepancies were noted between the officers' and the probationers' perception of the support and/or surveillance purposes of their supervision. These discrepancies, it emerged, were not based on either group's description of what they thought supervisory aims should be but rather on what, in their experience, they actually were.

The utility of the alternative concepts of support and surveillance in improving our understanding of the practice of the probation idea was also provisionally tested. The results were reported in the chapters which explored the themes of association, interaction, intervention and transformation and, without exception, the concepts proved to be extremely helpful in comprehending key features of the process of doing supervision. A few of the more striking examples serve to illustrate this. In the association chapter, for instance, the concepts were useful in not only identifying and explaining the reasons behind the different levels of contact between officers and probationers that were found but also how, in the officers' view, certain supervisory aims were better served by certain types of venue. Similarly, in the consideration of officer-probationer interaction, the concepts provided a helpful means of testing - and so far as the present sample is concerned rejecting - the long standing paradox that the supportive methods employed by officers to understand probationers were more likely to produce misunderstanding. However, probably the most graphic indication of the utility of support and surveillance and their improvement on care and control in comprehending the practice of the probation idea emerged in the next chapter from the critical incident analysis of helpful and harmful interventions. Here, it will be recalled, the sample was invited to apply the concepts of care and control to the various incidents they described in an attempt to assess their utility in elucidating the practice - if not the idea - of probation intervention. Once again however the concepts were found to manifest problems of inadequacy, conflation, confusion and prescription, whereas the concepts of support and surveillance offered a much more coherent and precise basis of classification.

In the presentation of these and other findings a detailed picture of probation practice has been described which, because of its complexity, inevitably precludes a satisfactory summary. Nevertheless, some important theoretical and practical implications for those engaged in either commentating on or doing supervision has been raised. For convenience they are presented below in the form of a series of questions and are intended as a guide for looking back at the analysis making them possible, as well as forward to future work that must necessarily be undertaken to clarify the position further.

Theoretical Implications

1. **In probation discourse, might care and control be better understood and appreciated as ideological rather than theoretical constructs?**

The distinction drawn here between ideology and theory as different types of social work knowledge is based on the following observation made by Loewenberg:

> Social science theory attempts to describe and explain <u>what is</u> while ideology is oriented toward <u>what ought to be</u>. Theory is made up of statements of rules and relationships, while ideology is based on values. The criteria for assessing theory are truth and validity, while the criteria for ideology are some person's notions of goodness.
> (1984 p. 320)

During the course of this book it has become increasingly relevant to ask whether probation educators, policymakers and practitioners are all engaged, when expressing their concern about caring and/or controlling, in referring to what ought to be rather than what is. This question was prompted initially because of the prescriptive use of the concepts by officers in the sample noted in Chapter 2. This ideological, as distinct from theoretical, usage is not especially surprising given, as was also reported in Chapter 2, first the immersion of probation practice within the realm of values, and second the open-ended nature of the care-control concepts. In both respects, the concepts' adoption within a variety of competing probation paradigms appears, if anything, inevitable. On the one hand, they provide a convenient shorthand for affirming the general value base of doing supervision, while on the other, they offer a means of signalling the particular values of the commentator/practitioner addressing them. If, as Loewenberg maintains, the operation of social work is such that it is important to identify and distinguish between the profession's ideology and theory, might the identification of care and control within probation discourse as ideological constructs serve to contribute to this important process of differentiation?

2. **How applicable is the concept of personalisation to an understanding of the probation officer's practice?**

This question is the result of two subordinate questions suggested by the findings which relate to the officers' aims and methods of supervision. First, is the process of personalisation a typical feature of doing supervision and second, if it is, where does personalisation end and agency constraint begin? The officers in the sample, it will be recalled from Chapter 2, rather than applying a monolithic theory of crime and a corresponding supervisory response to all of their cases, were invariably found to take each case to the various theories and responses at their disposal. This eclectic approach, where the diverse orientations were matched with the particular circumstances of the case, was conceptualised as the process of personalisation. In later chapters further evidence of this process was presented. In considering the theme of association, for example, no standardised level or composition of contact for particular officers, probationers or clusters of either group could be identified. Similarly, in the chapters concerned with the themes of interaction and intervention, a diverse range of conversations, critical incidents and levels of strictness were noted. In each of these instances the officers' methods of working seemed to make most sense in terms of their personalised response to the specific circumstances of the case, rather than reflecting a predetermined pattern of supervisory practice.

Further research is obviously needed to assess how typical these findings are but if they do mirror a widespread tendency among officers to personalise their practice, then this inquiry also suggests that the process is not an unlimited one. In the same chapters where examples of personalisation were noted, evidence was also found which indicated the possible influence of agency constraint upon it. For example, it is probably more than a coincidence that, although shared decision-making appeared to increase with the age of the order, neither the frequency nor the location of contact was ever decided by a probationer alone. Similarly, the presence of the non-reporting tariff administered by the officers irrespective of individual circumstances and their acknowledgement of the need to monitor and breach probationers where non-compliance with the terms of the order occurred, each contribute to an appreciation of the organisational boundaries within which the process of personalisation was seen to operate. Because the fieldwork reported here focused on relationships between officers and probationers rather than the influence of case committees and senior managers of the Probation Service on officers, the precise nature and extent of the boundaries remain insufficiently charted. Nevertheless, if it is the case that the concept of personalisation is considered applicable to an understanding of the probation officer's practice, then research which charts these boundaries would seem to be just as important as research which elucidates the personalisation process further.

Practical Implications

1. **Is inconsistency rather than incompatibility the major problem for probation support and surveillance?**

In this book differences between the support-surveillance and care-control paradigms have been suggested in relation to not only their theoretical precision but also the particular practical problems associated with them. Traditionally care-control commentaries have been concerned with the problem of incompatibility but the idea that support and surveillance would also contain antithetical objectives could not be substantiated. In the interaction chapter, for example, cases where a mixture of support and surveillance aims were identified were not associated with a greater degree of incomprehension or conflict than pure support or surveillance cases. It could not, therefore, be argued that the combination of support and surveillance objectives serve to generate either confusion or contradiction between officers and probationers. Similarly, it can be recalled how the vast majority of mixed support and surveillance interventions were evaluated positively by both groups and how none of the officers were constrained by what Bridges implied was a care-control dilemma of seeking to support probationers and then apply sanctions to them i.e. breaching, in the event of their persistent recalcitrance. The reasons for this compatibility appear from the evidence accrued here to be twofold, although further research will be necessary to confirm this. First, the justice and welfare orientations to support and surveillance, and second the process of personalisation whereby particular supervisory objectives and methods are matched to the particular circumstances of each case, both seem to provide for much more cohesiveness between the two overarching aims than has hitherto been formally recognised. This is not however to say that the implementation of support and surveillance was found to be unproblematic. At the close of Chapter 2 a new dilemma was suggested that arose from an inconsistency between what officers and probationers perceived as support and surveillance. Although the officers' accounts of their supervisory aims emphasised the contractual nature of their support and the non-punitiveness of their surveillance, many of the probationers questioned the amount of choice they had in forming a contract i.e. the support discrepancy, and regarded the purpose of the surveillance as being to punish them i.e. the surveillance discrepancy. If this inconsistency is a typical feature of probation practice, then it would seem to be as potentially undermining as the problem of incompatibility because it blurs the important line between statutory supervision as a distinctive alternative to custody as opposed to alternative form of custody. As Cohen has warned regarding the recent 'blurring' within the criminal justice system of the traditional boundaries between community and custodial supervision:

> the claim to be doing more good (or less harm) is somewhat less valid if the alternatives are not real alternatives at all, but supplements ... at the shallow end, the generation of new treatment criteria and the pervasiveness of the social welfare and preventive rhetorics, often ensure an erosion of traditional rights and liberties. (1985 p. 70)

Paradoxically, as later chapters exploring the methods and effects of supervision showed, in the vast majority of cases spontaneously negotiated - if not carefully prepared - contracts of help were evolved. Similarly, surveillance means were often seen as such and rarely degenerated into punitive ends in themselves. Nevertheless, this may be _in spite of_ rather than because of this inconsistency. The question therefore remains whether much of the dissension also documented in later chapters could have originated from the discrepant perception of support and surveillance by officers and probationers. Might much of the conflict and the strategies employed by the officers to manage it have been unnecessary if these discrepancies had been anticipated and addressed?

2. **Are two and three year probation and supervision orders too long?**

Approximately two-thirds of the sample received orders of two or three years length. This reflects a national trend which has persisted up to the current time (Home Office 1986 [b]). However, from examining the probationers' pattern of non-reporting, a statistically significant association was established between the duration of the supervision and the prevalence of missed appointments. This led to the impression that the older the order, the greater the likelihood of the supervision losing its sense of purpose and becoming counter-productive. Without the benefit of a controlled study of matched-probationers who have been subject to different lengths of supervision, any inferences from the present findings must be extremely tentative. Nevertheless, the findings here coupled with the promising results from research into short-term probation orders (Goldberg and Stanley, 1979), does raise the question of whether the quality of supervision is inversely related to its length. Therefore the implication for sentencers, practitioners and researchers that shorter orders than are customarily made may be more appropriate would seem to merit further attention and investigation from them.

3. Is the home the most suitable place for officers and juvenile probationers to have contact?

Although it has become conventional for social workers to see juvenile delinquency as 'appropriately explained by the family nexus' (Webb and Harris, 1984 p. 590), the analysis of venue preferences suggested that, so far as responding to juvenile delinquency is concerned, seeing juveniles in their home could often be inappropriate. While this type of environmental contact proved to be a useful means of accomplishing the assisting or monitoring objectives with all of the probationers, many of the juveniles were extremely unhappy about it; feeling either inhibited or spied on when seen at home. Consequently, a reappraisal of the advantages and disadvantages of home-based contact among those advocating a family-centred approach to juveniles would seem to be worthwhile.

4. Does the current enthusiasm for probation groupwork run a serious risk of obscuring the problems associated with the probationers' reluctance to undertake it?

Recently, discussions of groupwork in the probation setting have been concerned with its under development but the evidence presented in Chapter 3 has introduced a cautionary note regarding how it could be inappropriately over developed. For nearly two-thirds of those participating in various types of groups, mixed or wholly negative feelings were recorded. These, it emerged, were based mainly on the probationers' lack of confidence before and during their group contact. If as Monger claims, 'it hardly needs a sociologist to point out the importance to the average individual of the groups of which he is inevitably part' (1972 p. 186), nor also should it require a social psychologist to tell us that some average individuals find it harder than others to relate to groups. It may of course have been that the particular groups reviewed in the fieldwork were all badly run and are therefore unrepresentative. Only further research can clarify this and in the process perhaps assist practitioners in either avoiding or overcoming what seems to be an important problem facing the effective use of groupwork in probation practice.

5. **Is effective communication between officers and probationers dependent on the former's technical appreciation of and skill in utilising the latter's language?**

The work of Bernstein and Labov referred to in Chapter 4 showed that in the classroom context the absence of a common language between middle-class teachers and working-class pupils severely restricted the opportunities for engaging in meaningful conversation and learning. Effective communication in educational practice, it seems, is inhibited by the different linguistic codes and vernacular of the teachers and pupils. From the exploration of officer-probationer conversation and comprehension, particularly in relation to working-class juveniles, it appears - though further investigation is needed to confirm this - that the same can be said for probation practice. Although some of the officers were able to overcome this source of reticence many were unsuccessful, either because they lacked the necessary linguistic skills or, even more basically, an awareness of the problem. Perhaps therefore probation researchers, teachers and practitioners can enlist the help of their counterparts in the education field for assessing the extent of this communication problem in the probation context and, if appropriate, finding ways of dealing with it.

6. **Can conflict constitute a constructive element of probation interaction?**

Hitherto, active conflict during probation interaction has usually been regarded by commentators as something to be avoided because of its potentially destructive effect on the supervisory relationship. In the analysis of conflict reported in Chapter 4 however, the possibility of an alternative perspective was raised. This recalled Parkinson's comments some twenty years ago regarding the constructive potential of conflict between the officer and the probationer. Although the officers in the sample appeared to find the non-judgmental attitude useful in sustaining their supervisory relationships, they also indicated that through engaging in disagreements with their probationers the supervision was placed on a more realistic and effective footing.

7. **Do officers tend to be unrealistic about their supportive intervention?**

Barbara Wootton once remarked that the only feasible way for social workers to achieve their intimate and ambitious aims would be for them to marry their clients (1967 p. 273). A similar sort of observation might also be made of the officers in the sample because of the virtually unlimited support they expected themselves to provide and the very self-critical assessments they made of what they actually provided. The reader can recall, for example, the should-because-could-do-more attitude frequently expressed by the officers toward their supportive interventions, as well as their typically modest only-helpful assessments - compared with the really-helpful evaluations given by the probationers - of what they were able to accomplish. These tendencies, it was noted, closely resembled findings from previous research which suggest they are unlikely to be unrepresentative. If further research confirms this, then the implication would seem to be that ambitious aims and self-critical assessment are a double-edged sword. On the one hand they can serve to avoid complacency but on the other they can obscure what one commentator has argued as being the less glamorous but nonetheless important maintenance role of the social worker (Davies, 1981). In the maintenance role perspective, radical transformation of personality and society takes a back seat to the more mundane and pressing problems of everyday life; from having a shoulder to cry on to getting appointments to see D.H.S.S. and other officials. This is not to assert as Scull (1983) and others have that community supervision is nothing more than a superficial and cosmetic exercise but rather to offer some further empirical support for the recent and promising shift toward task-centred and time-limited interventions (Goldberg and Stanley op. cit. Singer 1983).

8.   Is stigma an extensive and insuperable problem for the probationer?

This research has provisionally suggested that for the probationer, stigma is neither extensive nor insuperable; though more detailed research is needed to assess the validity of such unexpected findings. In this connection, Walker's modified typology which was used as a basis for analysing stigma here, may prove to be a useful conceptual tool for future researchers. Moreover, it may also prove to be useful for present practitioners who want a practical checklist to periodically review the potentially negative effects which stem from being subject to statutory supervision. Indeed it might help them, if the findings here are representative, to identify what their sampled colleagues often seemed oblivious to; namely the problem of ostracism experienced by probationers. The potential for resolving this particular problem can be tentatively inferred from the evidence of constructive interventions made in relation to the other dimensions of stigma of which the officers in the sample were more aware. Although negative effects were also registered, the positive experiences noted, if nothing else, perhaps provide a useful rejoinder to the deterministic claim that the extensive manifestations of stigma can never be overcome.

Many of these theoretical and practical implications overlap but have been presented as separate questions for the sake of clarity. In future, the validity of posing them as well as the related propositions they may give rise to can perhaps be tested to a point where, in Merton's words, 'When propositions are logically inter-related, a theory has been instituted' (1968 p. 143).

APPENDIX

APPENDIX

PROBATIONER INTERVIEW GUIDE

INTRODUCTION

As you know from my letter, I'm writing a book about probation/supervision*. I want to talk to you to find out what it's really like. I'm going to talk to probation officers to ask them their views but I want to ask some people on probation/supervision* what their opinions are about it so that I get both sides of the picture. Before we start I want to assure you that whatever you say nobody but me will hear your answers. I have made it clear to your probation officer that on no account will I tell him/her* what you say and he/she has accepted this. When I write my book I will say something like 50% of the people on probation/supervision* I talked to thought this, while 50% thought that. So nobody will know who you are. I think that your views can help a great deal in finding out about probation/supervision* so please try and answer the questions as frankly and fully as you can. If you don't understand something, what I'm getting at, or a particular word, just say so. For the most part I'll ask you to tell me about things that you think are important. There aren't any right answers - any answer you give will be right providing you feel that it's right for you. Ok? Just to give you an idea of what I'm going to ask I start off by asking for some facts like how often you see your probation officer and then go on to ask you about your feelings and thoughts about this. I want to tape record our interview so that I don't have to keep stopping you to write down what you say. My questions should take just over an hour to answer. Before we begin, is there anything that you'd like to know? Can we begin then?

WHO I AM
(stress independence)

PURPOSE OF RESEARCH

CONFIDENTIALITY

FRANKNESS

IF YOU DON'T UNDERSTAND

NO RIGHT ANSWERS

WHAT I WILL ASK

TAPE RECORDER

INTERVIEW LENGTH
Stress that it is up to the respondent how long it lasts. If hour too long then give option for second session.

ANY QUESTIONS?

* delete as applicable

147

CONTACT SECTION

First of all I'd like to ask you about the sort of contact you've had with your probation officer since you started your probation order/supervision order. This will help me build a picture of how long, how often and where your contacts take place as well as what you feel and think about it. I'm really interested in two separate periods, namely the last three months, that is your latest contact, and the first three months of your order, that is your earliest contact. As we go along, you'll see how I've divided up the questions into these two separate periods. Ok? Right, I'll start the tape.

CHECK TIME AND START TAPE.

1A1 During the <u>last</u> three months of your probation/supervision order how often have you seen your probation officer?

(ALLOW FOR SUBJECTIVE IMPRESSION THEN SHOW PROMPT CARD 1 FOR OBJECTIVE CHECK)

So would you say more than once a week/once a week/once a fortnight/once a month?

(IF VARIES, RANK IN ORDER OF MOST TO LEAST FREQUENT)

1A2 Who decided that you would meet this often, the probation officer, you, or was it 50/50?

1A3 If the choice had been yours to make alone would you have seen your probation officer as often?

(ALLOW FOR SUBJECTIVE IMPRESSION THEN SHOW PROMPT CARD 2 FOR OBJECTIVE CHECK)

So would you say about the same/less often/more often/not at all?

(IF VARIES ETC)

1A4 (IF SAME) Does this mean that you're satisfied with the present arrangement, for example, that it is enough?

(IF DIFFERENT) Why is this?

1B1 How about during the <u>first</u> three months of your order, how often did you see your probation officer then?

(ALLOW FOR SUBJECTIVE IMPRESSION THEN SHOW PROMPT CARD 3 FOR OBJECTIVE CHECK)

So would you say more than once a week/once a week/once a fortnight/once a month?

(IF VARIES ETC)

1B2   Who decided that you would meet that often, the probation officer, you or was it 50/50?

1B3   If the choice had been yours to make alone, would you have gone to see your probation officer that often?

(ALLOW FOR SUBJECTIVE IMPRESSION THEN SHOW PROMPT CARD 4 FOR OBJECTIVE CHECK)

So would you say about the same/less often/more often/not at all?

1B4   (IF SAME) Does this mean that you were satisfied with the arrangement for those first three months? Was it enough, for example?

(IF DIFFERENT)   Why was this?

2A1   During the <u>last</u> three months how long have the interviews usually lasted?

(ALLOW FOR SUBJECTIVE IMPRESSION THEN SHOW PROMPT CARD 5 FOR OBJECTIVE CHECK)

So would you say under 15 minutes/15-30 minutes/30-45 minutes/45-60 minutes/over an hour?

(IF VARIES ETC)

2A2   Has this been long enough, too little or too much?

2A3   (IF ENOUGH) Does this mean that you're satisfied with the present arrangement?

(IF OTHER) Can you tell me why you say too little/much?

2B1   How about during the <u>first</u> three months of your order? How long did the interviews usually last then?

(ALLOW FOR SUBJECTIVE IMPRESSION THEN SHOW PROMPT CARD 6 FOR OBJECTIVE CHECK)

So would you say under 15 minutes/15-30 minutes/30-45 minutes/45-60 minutes/over an hour?

(IF VARIES ETC)

2B2   Was this long enough, too little or too much?

2B3   (IF ENOUGH) Does this mean that you were satisfied with the arrangement?

(IF OTHER) Can you tell me why you say too little/much?

3A1   During the <u>last</u> three months where have you usually seen your probation officer?

(ALLOW FOR SUBJECTIVE IMPRESSION THEN SHOW PROMPT CARD 7 FOR OBJECTIVE CHECK)

So would you say probation office/your home/work/school/local club or pub/probation officer's home/anywhere else (specify)?

(IF VARIES ETC)

3A2 Who decided where you would meet, the probation officer, you, or was it 50/50?

3A3 If the choice has been left up to you alone, do you think this (these) is (are) where you would have decided (liked/wanted) to usually meet?

3A4 (IF SAME) Does this mean that you're satisfied with the arrangement?

(IF DIFFERENT) Where would you meet and why is this?

3B1 Going back to your early contact, during the first three months where did you usually see your probation officer then?

(ALLOW FOR SUBJECTIVE IMPRESSION THEN SHOW PROMPT CARD 8 FOR OBJECTIVE CHECK)

So would you say probation office/your home/work/school/local club or pub/probation officer's home/anywhere else (specify)?

(IF VARIES ETC)

3B2 Who decided where you would meet then, the probation officer, you or was it 50/50?

3B3 If during those first three months the choice had been left up to you alone, do you think this (these) is (are) where you would have decided (liked/wanted) to usually meet?

3B4 (IF SAME) Does this mean that you were satisfied with the arrangement?

(IF DIFFERENT) Where would you have met and why is this?

4A1 During the last three months have you ever missed any appointments to see your probation officer?

4A2 (IF YES) Can you tell me briefly what happened, why was this, what did your probation officer do or say about it, and do you think it mattered?

(IF NO) Do you think it would have mattered if you had?

4B1 During the first three months did you ever miss any appointments then to see your probation officer?

4B2   (IF YES) Can you briefly tell me what happened, why was this, what did your probation officer do or say about it and do you think it mattered?

(IF NO) Do you think it would have mattered then if you had?

PURPOSES AND INCIDENTS SECTION

As I told you, the aim of the interview is to find out about your views and experiences of probation/supervision. In order to do this I want now to move on from questions about the amount of contact you've had to questions about what actually goes on. But first of all I'll ask you some questions on your thoughts about the purpose of probation/supervision, like what you think the point of it is. Ok?

5A*   First of all then can you tell me what you think the purpose of probation/supervision really is?

5B*   Do you think probation/supervision is more to do with either caring about you as an individual with some personal difficulties or controlling what you do or say so that you don't misbehave? Or is it a mixture of both? (CHECK IN WHAT WAY)

6   What do you think your probation officer thinks the purpose of probation/supervision is?

7   What do you think he/she believes being on probation/supervision should do for you?

8   How does he/she try to achieve this, for example, what does he/she do or say?

9   What do you think being on probation/supervision should do for you?

10   What difference has probation/supervision made to you? (GET THEM TO ASSESS WHETHER THE DIFFERENCE WAS MAJOR, MEDIUM OR MINOR, AND IN WHAT WAY)

11   Do you think your probation/supervision could be (or could have been) improved in any way? (SPECIFY)

*   During the first interview officers were invited to relate their thoughts on the purpose of probation and supervision in general as well as the nature and applicability of the concepts of care and control as a designation of supervisory aims.

HELPFUL - HARMFUL INCIDENTS

12A1 Can you tell me now about things your probation officer has done or said since you've been on probation/supervision that <u>you</u> think have been really helpful or really harmful?

(ALLOW RESPONDENT TO RELATE AS MANY INCIDENTS AS TIME ALLOWS EITHER HELPFUL OR HARMFUL, AS THEY OCCUR, ENCOURAGING THE NARRATIVE BUT <u>NOT</u> GUIDING. FOR EACH SEPARATE INCIDENT CLARIFY:

WHAT EXACTLY HAPPENED.

HOW IT OCCURRED.

WHAT THE PROBATION OFFICER SAID AND/OR DID.

WHAT THE RESPONDENT SAID AND/OR DID.

THE CONNECTION TO THE SUPERVISORY AIMS.

WHAT THE OUTCOME WAS).

12A2 Overall then, would you say that your probation officer was mainly caring about you as an individual with some personal difficulty <u>or</u> controlling what you did or said so that you didn't misbehave? Or was it a mixture of the two? (CHECK IN WHAT WAY)

13A1 (IF RESPONDENT NEEDS PROMPTING)

I have here a list of certain people, places and things which you and your probation officer may have covered since the start of your order. I'll go through the list with you and what I'd like to know is if you can think of something that your probation officer did or said which was connected with one of these people, places or things which <u>you</u> think was either helpful, harmful or possibly a mixture of both. Here's the list (SHOW PROMPT CARD 9 BELOW)

SINCE YOU STARTED YOUR ORDER HAS YOUR PROBATION OFFICER DONE OR SAID ANYTHING CONNECTED WITH ANY OF THESE PEOPLE, PLACES OR THINGS WHICH YOU THINK WERE EITHER HELPFUL, HARMFUL OR A MIXTURE OF BOTH?

<u>WORK</u> - LIKE FINDING A JOB, KEEPING IT OR GETTING ON WITH WORKMATES
<u>SCHOOL</u> - LIKE GETTING ON WITH TEACHERS, LESSONS OR SCHOOLMATES
<u>MONEY</u> - LIKE RENT, HIRE PURCHASE, SOCIAL SECURITY OR SPENDING MONEY
<u>ACCOMMODATION</u> - LIKE FINDING, FIXING UP OR KEEPING A PLACE TO LIVE
<u>YOUR PERSONAL LIFE</u> - LIKE FEELING DEPRESSED OR NOT BEING ABLE TO COPE
<u>HOW THINGS ARE WITH YOU AND</u> - YOUR GIRLFRIEND/WIFE, BOYFRIEND/HUSBAND
<u>HOW THINGS ARE WITH YOU AND</u> - YOUR FAMILY
<u>PROBLEMS WITH</u> - DRINKING OR DRUGTAKING OR GAMBLING
<u>KEEPING AWAY FROM</u> - CERTAIN PEOPLE
<u>KEEPING AWAY FROM</u> - CERTAIN PLACES
<u>GETTING INTO FURTHER TROUBLE</u> - LIKE WITH THE POLICE OR COURTS
SOMETHING ELSE - ....

13A2   Overall then ... (AS IN 12A2)

PROBATION OFFICER - PROBATION/SUPERVISIONER RELATIONSHIP SECTION

I'd like now to ask you a few questions about how you get on with your probation officer.

14A   First, have you ever seen any other probation officer when your usual one has not been available?

(IF YES, PROBE BRIEFLY WHO, WHEN, WHAT HAPPENED, AND FEELINGS ABOUT SEEING SOMEONE ELSE)

14B   How would you feel about having to change to another probation officer?

15A   When you see your usual probation officer, is there anyone else present?

15B   (IF YES, PROBE BRIEFLY WHO, WHEN, WHY AND FEELINGS ABOUT INVOLVING SOMEONE ELSE)

16A   during your meetings with your probation officer, who would you say does the most talking, the probation officer, you, or is it 50/50?   (IF VARIES ETC).

16B   How do you feel about this?

17A   What are the main things that the two of you talk about in your meetings?

17B   Are you conversations varied, or do you think you've got into a rut?

18A   Can you understand what your probation officer talks about, what he/she is getting at?

18B   (WHETHER YES, NO, OR SOMETIMES ASK) Can you give me an example?

19A   How about the other way round? Do you think your probation officer understands what you're talking about?

19B   (WHETHER YES, NO, OR SOMETIMES) Can you give me an example?

20A   Have you ever disagreed with your probation officer about what you should or shouldn't do?   (IF SO)   Can you give me an example?

20B   Do you feel that you can strongly disagree with your probation officer? (WHETHER YES, NO OR SOMETIMES, ASK FOR EXAMPLE)

21A   Which other person in your life does your probation officer remind you of?

21B   Why is that?

22A I have here a list of people. Which two of them do you think your probation officer is most like? (SHOW AND READ PROMPT CARD 10)

COURT-OFFICIAL/ FOREMAN/ POLICEMAN/ PRIEST-OR-MINISTER/ PSYCHIATRIST/ TEACHER/ WELFARE-OFFICER

22B In what way?

23A Here's another list of people. Which two of these would you say your probation officer is most like? (SHOW AND READ PROMPT CARD 11)

BUSYBODY/FRIEND/INTERESTED-OUTSIDER/NOSY-PARKER/ONE-OF-THE FAMILY/ONE-OF-"THEM"/STRANGER

23B In what way?

PERCEPTIONS OF OFFENCE BEHAVIOUR SECTION

I want now to ask you about the events leading up to your being placed on probation/supervision and your thoughts about it.

24 To start, can you tell me a little bit about the offence which led to your being placed on probation/supervision? I'm interested in what and how it happened.

25 If someone asked your probation officer what it was about you that caused you to get into trouble, what do you think he/she would say?

(ALLOW OPEN ENDED RESPONSE IF FORTHCOMING. THEN FOLLOW UP WITH)

26 Here are four things your probation officer might say about the reason you got into trouble. (SHOW PROMPT CARD 12 AND READ. GO THROUGH ALL OF THEM SO RESPONDENT KNOWS WHAT THEY ARE AND THEN SEPARATELY TO ENSURE HE/SHE UNDERSTANDS EACH OF THEM)

WHICH OF THESE FOUR THINGS DO YOU THINK YOUR PROBATION OFFICER MIGHT SAY ABOUT THE REASON YOU GOT INTO TROUBLE:

A. ALTHOUGH YOU KNEW THE LAW, YOUR FEELINGS AND THOUGHTS WERE MIXED UP BECAUSE OF PERSONAL PROBLEMS AND YOU COULDN'T HELP YOURSELF.

B. SOME PEOPLE YOU KNEW EXPECTED YOU TO OBEY THE LAW WHILE OTHERS EXPECTED YOU TO BREAK IT AND IT WAS HARD TO KNOW WHAT WAS RIGHT TO DO.

C. YOU BELIEVED IN DECIDING FOR YOURSELF WHAT WAS RIGHT AND WRONG AND IT JUST TURNED OUT THAT THIS LED TO YOUR DOING SOMETHING WHICH BROKE SOME LAW.

D. YOU DECIDED TO TAKE A CHANCE AND WERE UNLUCKY GETTING CAUGHT DOING WHAT EVERYBODY ELSE DOES OR WOULD DO GIVEN THE OPPORTUNITY.

(AFTER GOING THROUGH THESE FOUR TOGETHER AND SEPARATELY ASK)

E. OR DO YOU THINK HE'D/SHE'D SAY SOMETHING ENTIRELY DIFFERENT?

27 If I ask you what it is about you that caused you to get into trouble what, in your own words, would you say??

28 How about the four things on the card? (REFER TO PROMPT CARD 12)

29 OK I want to move on a bit. When you went to court what did you think the magistrate/judge would decided to do with you, what kind of result or sentence did you expect?

(IF NECESSARY, SHOW PROMPT CARD 13)

NOT-GUILTY/CONDITIONAL-DISCHARGE/FINE/SUSPENDED-SENTENCE/PROBATION/CUSTODY/SOMETHING ELSE.

30A Was a social enquiry report carried out before judgment?

30B (IF SO) Was there a recommendation?

30C (IF SO) What was it?

30D How did you feel about it (PROBE FOR DETAILS INCLUDING HOW IT AFFECTED RELATIONSHIP WITH SERVICE/OFFICER)

31 (IF APPLICABLE, IE NOT COVERED BY 30) What did you feel like when the court decided to place you on probation/supervision?

32 What did you think it would be like being on probation/supervision? (PROBE FOR DETAILS)

33 Do you still think this now? (PROBE FOR DETAILS)

34A Since the start of your probation/supervision order have you had any further trouble with the police or the courts?
(IF YES, PROBE FOR DETAILS OF:-
WHAT HAPPENED
WHY
WHAT PROBATION OFFICER SAID AND/OR DID
HIS/HER VIEW OF CAUSES
WHAT RESPONDENT SAID AND/OR DID
HIS/HER VIEW OF CAUSES (FOR JUVENILES CHECK SCHOOL TROUBLE))

34B (IF NO) Is that because you have been honest or just lucky not to get caught?

GENERAL IMPRESSIONS AND ATTITUDES SECTION

Lastly I want to finish up by asking you some general questions about your overall contacts with your probation officer and experiences of probation/supervision. Ok?

35   First then, looking back over all your contacts and experiences with your probation officer do you think you're getting anywhere? (WHETHER YES, NO OR MIXED, CHECK IN WHAT WAY)

36A1   Here is what I call a strictness scale (SHOW PROMPT CARD 14). It's in two parts: strictness so far as things said goes, and strictness so far as things done goes. When it comes to things said or things done some probation officers are very strict, others are very easy going. How would you rate your probation officer on this scale? What about "things said". Is he/she:-

1. VERY STRICT.........<u>ALWAYS</u> TELLS ME WHAT I MUST OR MUSTN'T DO
2. STRICT..............<u>MOSTLY</u> TELLS ME WHAT I MUST OR MUSTN'T DO
3. MODERATE............<u>SOMETIMES</u> TELLS ME WHAT I MUST/MUSTN'T DO
4. EASY GOING..........<u>RARELY</u> TELLS ME WHAT I MUST OR MUSTN'T DO
5. VERY EASY GOING.....<u>NEVER</u> TELLS ME WHAT I MUST OR MUSTN'T DO

36A2   Regarding "things said" has the fact of your probation officer being strict/easy going been helpful or harmful?

36A3   Can you give me an example?

36B1   How about strictness and "things done"? Is he/she:-

1. VERY STRICT..........<u>ALWAYS</u> CHECKS UP ON WHERE I'M LIVING OR WORKING OR SPENDING MY SPARE TIME.
2. STRICT...............<u>MOSTLY</u> CHECKS UP ON WHERE I'M LIVING OR WORKING OR SPENDING MY SPARE TIME.
3. MODERATE.............<u>SOMETIMES</u> CHECKS UP ON WHERE I'M LIVING/ WORKING OR SPENDING MY SPARE TIME.
4. EASY GOING...........<u>RARELY</u> CHECKS UP ON WHERE I'M LIVING OR WORKING OR SPENDING MY SPARE TIME.
5. VERY EASY GOING......<u>NEVER</u> CHECKS UP ON WHERE I'M LIVING OR WORKING OR SPENDING MY SPARE TIME.

36B2   Regarding 'things done' has the fact of your probation officer being strict/easy going been helpful or harmful?

36B3   Can you give me an example?

37A*   Has your probation officer ever warned you about, or actually taken you back to court for breaking the rules of your Order? (IF SO, CLARIFY WHAT HAPPENED AND WHY, THEN ASK) What did you think and feel about this?

37B   (IF NOT, ASK WHAT THEY THINK AND FEEL ABOUT THE POWER TO BREACH)

*   During the first interview, officers were asked to relate their general thoughts and feelings about the practice of breaching.

38A   How important a part has supervision played in your life?
      (ALLOW FOR SUBJECTIVE IMPRESSION THEN SHOW PROMPT CARD 15)

      How would you rate the importance of supervision in your life on this scale?

1.   SUPERVISION HAS ALWAYS   BEEN IMPORTANT TO WHAT I'VE DONE

2.   SUPERVISION HAS MOSTLY   BEEN IMPORTANT TO WHAT I'VE DONE

3.   SUPERVISION HAS SOMETIMES BEEN IMPORTANT TO WHAT I'VE DONE

4.   SUPERVISION HAS RARELY   BEEN IMPORTANT TO WHAT I'VE DONE

5.   SUPERVISION HAS NEVER   BEEN IMPORTANT TO WHAT I'VE DONE

38B   Has the fact that supervision has been always never important been helpful or harmful?

38C   In what way has it been helpful/harmful?

39A   How many of the people you come into contact with know you are on probation/supervision?
      (SHOW PROMPT CARD 16)
      So would you say All/Most/Some/Few/None

39B   Has the fact that ... of the people you come into contact with know you are on probation/supervision been helpful or harmful??

39C   In what way has it been helpful/harmful? (GET EXAMPLES)

40A* If you were a probation officer what changes would you make to improve the job? (PROBE FOR DETAILS AND REASONS)

40B* On the other hand, what features would you keep? (PROBE ATTITUDE TOWARD STATUTORY CONDITIONS, REPORTING AND HOME VISITING)

41A* If you were in a position to decide, what kinds of people would you put on probation/supervision?

      (PROBE TYPES OF OFFENDERS AND TYPES OF OFFENCES)

41B* On the other hand, what kinds of people wouldn't you put on probation/supervision?

      (PROBE TYPES OF OFFENDERS AND TYPES OF OFFENCES)

Well, that's all I have to ask so, unless there's anything I haven't asked which you think that I should have, we can stop now.

(IF NOTHING, STOP TAPE AND CHECK TIME. CLOSE INTERVIEW BY THANKING RESPONDENT AND ASSURING THAT ALL INFORMATION WILL BE TREATED CONFIDENTIALLY)

*   These items were covered with the officer during the first interview.

Bibliography

Anderson, B., 1981, 'The Intuitive Response', Probation Journal, vol. 28, no. 2.

Axon, L., 1977, 'Probation Officers', Accounts of Their Office Supervision of Offenders', Unpublished Cambridge Univ. Ph.D thesis.

Baldock, J. & Prior, D., 1981, 'Social Workers Talking to Clients: A Study of Verbal Behaviour', Brit. Jrnl. of Social Work, 11.

Barr, H., 1966, A Survey of Group Work In the Probation Service, Home Office Research Unit, Report No. 9, H.M.S.O.

Bateson, G. et al, 1956, 'Toward a Theory of Schizophrenia', of Schizophrenia', Behavioural Science, 1.

Becker, H., 1963, Outsiders: Studies in the Sociology of Deviance, Free Press.

Bernstein, B., 1971, Class, Codes and Control, Vol. 1, Routledge and Kegan Paul.

Biestek, F., 1974, The Casework Relationship, Unwin Univ.Books.

Blackburn, R. (ed.), 1972, Ideology in the Social Sciences, Fontana.

Blake, B. & Godson, D., 1982, 'Re-Thinking "Sentenced to Social Work?" ', Probation Journal, Vol. 29, No. 4.

Bochel, D., 1976, Probation and After Care, Scottish Academic Press.

Boswell, G., 1985, *Care, Control and Accountability in the Probation Service*, Social Work Monographs 29, Univ. East Anglia.

Bottoms, A. & McWilliams, W., 1979, 'A Non Treatment Paradigm for Probation Practice', *Brit. Jrnl. of Social Work*, 9, 2.

Bridges, D., 1976, *Section Six*, West Yorkshire Probation Service.

Bryant, M. et al, 1978, 'Sentenced to Social Work'?, *Probation Journal*, Vol. 25, No. 4.

Butrym, Z., 1982, *The Nature of Social Work*, Macmillan.

Cain, M., 1979, 'The General Practice Lawyer and the Client: Towards a Radical Conception', *Int. Jrnl. Sociology of Law*, Vol. 7, No. 4.

Carlen, P., 1976, *Magistrates' Justice*, Martin Robertson.

Carver, M., 1974, 'Relationships in Probation', Unpublished Home Office Research Unit Report.

Central Council for Education & Training in Social Work (CCETSW)., 1975, *Education and Training for Social Work*, Paper 10, CCETSW.

CCETSW., 1976, *Values in Social Work*, Paper 13, CCETSW.

CCETSW., 1978, *Learning to be a Probation Officer*, Paper 18, CCETSW.

Clifton, J., 1981, 'Social Workers Talking to Clients: A Comment', *Brit. Jrnl. of Social Work*, 11.

Cohen, L. & Holliday, M., 1983, *Statistics for Social Scientists*, Harper and Row.

Cohen, S., 1975, 'It's Alright for You to Talk' in Bailey, R. & Brake, M. (eds.), *Radical Social Work*, Edward Arnold.

Cohen, S., 1985, *Visions of Social Control*, Polity Press.

Crolley, T. & Paley, J., 1983, 'Probation Officers and the "Intelligent" Client', *Probation Journal*, Vol. 30, No. 1.

Davies, M., 1969, *Probationers in their Social Environment*, Home Office Research Unit Report No. 2, H.M.S.O.

Davies, M., 1972, 'The Objectives of the Probation Service', *Brit. Jrnl. of Social Work*, Vol. 2, No. 3.

Davies, M., 1979, 'Through the Eyes of the Probationer', *Probation Journal*, Vol. 26, No. 3.

Davies, M., 1981, *The Essential Social Worker*, Heinemann.

Davies, M. et al, 1974, *Social Work in the Environment*, Home Office Research Unit Report No. 21, H.M.S.O.

Day, P., 1981, *Social Work and Social Control*, Tavistock.

Denzin, N., 1970, The Research Act in Sociology, Butterworths.

Ericson, R., 1977, 'Social Distance and Reaction to Criminality', Brit. Jrnl. Criminology, Vol. 17, No. 1.

Erikson, K., 1964, 'Notes on the Sociology of Deviance', in Becker, H. (ed.) the other side, Free Press.

Folkard, S. et al, 1966, Probation Research: a Preliminary Note, Home Office Research Unit, H.M.S.O.

Folkard, S. et al, 1974, Intensive Matched Probation and After Care Treatment: Volume 1, Home Office Research Study No. 24, H.M.S.O.

Folkard, S. et al, 1976, I.M.P.A.C.T. Vol. II: The Results of the Experiment, Home Office Research Study No. 36, H.M.S.O.

Foren, W. & Bailey, R., 1968, Authority in Social Casework, Pergamon Press.

Foucault, M., 1977, Discipline and Punish, Penguin Books.

Fowler, D., 1976, 'Can Control Be Justified?', in King, J. (ed.), Control Without Custody, Cambridge Univ. Press.

Furlong, V., 1976, 'Interaction Sets in the Classroom', in Stubbs, M. & Delamont, S. (eds.), Explorations in Classroom Observation, Wiley.

Gahagan, J., 1984, Social Interaction and its Management, Methuen.

Garfinkel, H., 1956, 'Conditions of Successful Degradation Ceremonies', American Journal of Sociology, LXIV.

Giller, H. & Morris, A., 1978, 'Supervision Orders: The Routinization of Treatment', Howard Journal, Vol. 17, No. 3.

Goffman, E., 1967, Interaction Ritual, Penguin Books.

Goffman, E., 1984, The Presentation of Self in Everyday Life, Penguin Books.

Goldberg, E. & Stanley, S., 1979, 'A Task Centred Approach to Probation', in King, J. (ed.), Pressures and Changes in the Probation Service, Cambridge Univ. Press.

Goldberg, E. & Warburton, R., 1979, Ends and Means in Social Work, Allen and Unwin.

Gouldner, A., 1977, The Coming Crisis of Western Sociology, Heinemann.

Griffiths, W., 1982, 'Supervision in the Community', Justice of the Peace, 21st August.

Hardiker, P., 1975, 'Ideologies in Social Inquiry Reports', Final Progress Report to the Social Science Research Council.

Hardiker, P., 1979, 'The Role of Probation Officers in Sentencing', in Parker, H. (ed.), Social Work and the Courts, Arnold.

Hardiker, P. & Webb, D., 1979, 'Explaining Deviant Behaviour: The Social Context of 'Action' and 'Infraction' Accounts in the Probation Service', Sociology, 13.

Harris, R., 1977, 'The Probation Officer as Social Worker, Brit. Jrnl. of Social Work, 7,4.

Harris, R., 1980, 'A Changing Service: The Case for Separating 'Care' and 'Control' in Probation Practice', Brit. Jrnl. of Social Work, 10.

Heron, J., 1982, 'A Six Category Intervention Analysis' in Bolger, A. (ed.), Counselling in Britain, Batsford Academic.

Home Office., 1970, Report on the Work of the Prison Department 1969, H.M.S.O.

Home Office., 1977, A Review of Criminal Justice Policy 1976, H.M.S.O.

Home Office., 1982, Probation and After Care Statistics England and Wales 1981, Government Statistical Service, H.M.S.O.

Home Office., 1984(a), Criminal Justice: A Working Paper, H.M.S.O.

Home Office., 1984(b), 'Statement of National Objectives and Priorities', Home Office, April 30th.

Home Office., 1986(a), 'Reconvictions of Those Given Probation Orders', Home Office Statistical Bulletin, 10th November, 1986, Government Statistical Service.

Home Office., 1986(b), Probation Statistics England and Wales 1984, Government Statistical Service H.M.S.O.

Honnard, R. & Sanfilippo, R., 1961, 'Incidents: Probationers' Descriptions', in McEachern, A. (ed.), Views of Authority: Youth Studies Centre, Los Angeles.

Hood, R. & Sparks, R., 1974, Key Issues in Criminology, World University Library.

Hunt, A., 1966, 'Enforcement in Probation Casework', Brit. Jrnl. Criminology, Vol. 4, No. 3.

Jamieson, J., 1978, 'What is an Interview'?, Community Care, February 8th.

Jarvis, F., 1980, Probation Officer's Manual, Third Edition, Butterworths.

King, J. (ed.), 1969, The Probation and After Care Service, Third Edition, Butterworths.

Kirwin, K., 1985, 'Probation and Supervision' in Walker, H. & Beaumont, B. (eds.), Working with Offenders, Macmillan.

Kittrie, N., 1972, The Right to be Different, Baltimore, Md, Penguin Books.

Kuhn, T., 1970, The Structure of Scientific Revolutions, Second Edition, Univ. Chicago Press.

Lacey, A., 1976, A Dictionary of Philosophy, Routledge and Kegan Paul.

Labov, W., 1969, 'The Logic of Non Standard English', Georgetown Monographs on Language and Linguistics. Vol. 22.

Lawson, C., 1978, The Probation Officer as Prosecutor, Institute of Criminology, Occasional Papers No. 3, Cambridge Univ. Press.

Lemert, E., 1967, Human Deviance, Social Problems and Social Control, Prentice Hall.

Le Mesurier, L. (ed.), 1935, A Handbook of Probation, National Association of Probation Officers.

Limont, W., 1976, 'The Probation and After Care Service and the Courts', Probation Journal, Vol. 23, No. 2.

Loewenberg, F., 1984, 'Progessional Ideology, Middle Range Theories and Knowledge Building for Social Work Practice', Brit. Jrnl. of Social Work, 14.

McBarnet, D., 1978, 'False Dichotomies in Criminal Justice Research', in Baldwin, J. & Bottomley, A. (eds.), Criminal Justice, Martin Robertson.

McEachern, A. et al, 1961, Views of Authority: Probationers and Probation Officers, Youth Studies Centre, Univ. S. California, Los Angeles.

Mathieson, D., 1976, 'A Philosophy of Reconciliation', Probation Journal, Vol. 23, No. 3.

Mayer, J. & Timms, N., 1970, The Client Speaks, Routledge and Kegan Paul.

Mead, G., 1918, 'The Psychology of Punitive Justice', American Jrnl. of Sociology, 23.

Merton, R., 1968, Social Theory and Social Structure, Enlarged Edition, Free Press.

Monger, M., 1972, Casework in Probation, Butterworths.

Morison, R. Chairman, 1962, Report of the Departmental Committee on the Probation Service, Cmnd. 1650.

Mucchielli, R., 1983, *Face to Face in the Counselling Interview*, Macmillan.

Nelson-Jones, R., 1983, *Practical Counselling Skills*, Holt Reinhart and Winston.

Parker, H., 1979, 'Client Defendant Perceptions of Juvenile and Criminal Justice', in Parker, H. (ed.), *Social Work and the Courts*, Arnold.

Parker, H. et al, 1981, *Receiving Juvenile Justice*, Blackwell.

Parkinson, G., 1966, 'Passivity and Delinquency', *Probation Journal*, Vol. 12, No. 2.

Parkinson, G., 1970, 'I Give Them Money', *New Society*, March 31st.

Parkinson, G., 1977(a), 'Probation by Stealth', *New Society*, March 31st.

Parkinson, G., 1977(b), 'Really He Was a Goody All the Time', *Social Work Today*, 6,1.

Parsloe, P., 1967, *The Work of the Probation Officer*, Routledge and Kegan Paul.

Parsloe, P., 1976, 'Social Work and the Justice Model' *Brit. Jrnl. of Social Work* 6, 1.

Parsloe, P., 1979, 'Issues of Social Control', in King, J. (ed.), *Pressures and Changes in the Probation Service*, Cambridge Univ. Press.

Plummer, K., 1979, 'Misunderstanding Labelling Perspectives', in Downes, D. & Rock, P. *Deviant Interpretations*, Martin Robertson.

Raynor, P., 1978, 'Compulsory Persuasion: A Problem for Correctional Social Work', *Brit. Jrnl. of Social Work*, 8, 4.

Rubington, E. & Weinburg, M. (eds.), 1973, *Deviance: The Interactionist Perspective*, Third Edition, Macmillan.

Sainsbury, E. et al, 1982, *Social Work in Focus*, Routledge and Kegan Paul.

Satyamurti, C., 1981, *Occupational Survival*, Blackwell.

Scott, M., 1968, *The Racing Game*, Chicago, Aldine.

Scull, A., 1983, 'Community Corrections: Panacea, Progress or Pretence'?, in Garland, D. &. Young, P. (eds.) *The Power to Punish*, Heinemann.

Sharron, H., 1984, 'Hunted or Helped'?, *Social Work Today*, October 22nd.

Sheppard, B., 1980, 'Research Into Aspects of Probation', *Research Bulletin* No. 10, Home Office Research Unit.

Siegel, S., 1956, *Non-Parametric Statistics for the Social Sciences*, McGraw-Hill.

Simmel, G., 1908, 'Conflict as Sociation', in Coser, L. & Rosenberg, B. (eds.) 1976, *Sociological Theory*, Fifth Edition, Collier Macmillan.

Singer, L., 1983, *Trouble Through Drink: An Evaluation of the Reading Alcohol Study Group*, Berkshire Council on Alcoholism & Berkshire Probation Service.

Thorpe, D. et al, 1980, *Out of Care: The Community Support of Juvenile Offenders*, George Allen and Unwin.

Timms, N., 1964, *Social Casework*, Routledge and Kegan Paul.

Timms, N., 1968, *Language of Social Casework*, Routledge and Kegan Paul.

Timms, N. & Timms, R., 1977, *Perspectives in Social Work*, Routledge Kegan Paul.

Tutt, N., 1982, 'Justice or Welfare'?, *Social Work Today*, Vol. 14, No. 7.

Walker, H. & Beaumont, B., 1981, *Probation Work: Critical Theory and Socialist Practice*, Blackwell.

Walker, N., 1980, *Punishment, Danger and Stigma*, Blackwell.

Webb, D. & Harris, R., 1984, 'Social Workers and Supervision Orders: A Case of Occupational Uncertainty', *Brit. Jrnl. of Social Work*, 14.

Weber, M., 1949, *The Methodology of the Social Sciences*, trans. Shils, E. & Finch, H., Free Press.

Weber, M., 1964, *The Theory of Social and Economic Organisation*, Free Press.

Winch, P., 1976, *The Idea of a Social Science and its Relation to Philosopy*, Routledge and Kegan Paul.

Winnicott, C., 1962, 'Casework and Agency Function' *Case Conference*, Vol. 8, No. 7.

Worrall, A., 1981, 'Out of Place: Female Offenders in Court', *Probation Journal*, Vol. 28, No. 3.

Wootton, B., 1967, *Social Science and Social Pathology*, George Allen and Unwin.

Younger, K., 1974, 'Introducing the Report', *Probation Journal*, Vol. 21, No. 4.